Spiritual Doctrine Of
BLESSED ELIZABETH OF THE TRINITY

Spiritual Doctrine Of
BLESSED ELIZABETH OF THE TRINITY

APOSTOLIC CONTEMPLATIVE

by

LUIGI BORRIELLO, O.C.D.

translated by

Jordan Aumann, O.P.

ALBA · HOUSE   NEW · YORK

SOCIETY OF ST. PAUL, 2187 VICTORY BLVD., STATEN ISLAND, NEW YORK 10314

Library of Congress Cataloging in Publication Data

Borriello, Luigi
 The spiritual doctrine of Blessed Elizabeth of the Trinity

 Translation of: Elisabetta della Trinità.
 Includes biblographical references.
 1. Elisabeth de la Trinité, soeur, 1880-1906.
2 Carmelite Nuns — France — Biography. 3. Mystics —
France — Biography. I. Title.

BX4705.E44B6713   1986   248.2   86-3446
ISBN 0-8189-0500-X

---

*Designed, printed and bound in the United States of
America by the Fathers and Brothers of the
Society of St. Paul, 2187 Victory Boulevard,
Staten Island, New York 10314, as part of their
communications apostolate.*

---

3 4 5 6 7 8 9 (Current Printing: first digit)

Translated from the Italian work
entitled
ELISABETTA DELLA TRINITÀ:
Una Vocazione Realizzata secondo il Progetto di Dio,
published by Edizioni Dehoniane,
Naples, 1980.

PREFACE

ON THE OCCASION of the centenary of the birth of the Servant of God, Sister Elizabeth of the Trinity (1880-1906), Father Luigi Borriello, O.C.D., presented the interior richness of this modern mystic in an organic and orderly manner. His is an original work that highlights the various stages of the spiritual journey of the Carmelite of Dijon, centered as it was on the mystery of the indwelling of the Blessed Trinity in her soul.

In the development of this essential nucleus of Elizabeth's interior life, the author brings out certain predominant characteristics such as "called by name" — Elizabeth, meaning "house of God"; the presence of Mary, the attentive Virgin (listening); configuration with Christ, dead and resurrected.

Father Borriello's work becomes ever more relevant as he traces the similarity between the doctrine of Sister Elizabeth and the teaching of Vatican Council II. As a result of this comparison, the Carmelite of Dijon is seen as a "forerunner of the ideas promoted by the Council and of a new manner of being the Church and in the Church as a contemplative and an apostle."

The experience of communion with the Trinity as the mystery of loving dialogue, of authentic life to be lived in depth in the ordinary occupations of daily life and, finally, of the witness of an existence spent in love — all this is perceived and presented by Elizabeth as the vocation of the entire Church, which vocation "will always have an honored place in the mystical body of Christ, . . . no matter how pressing may be the needs of the active ministry.

Contemplatives offer to God an exceptional sacrifice of praise, they lend luster to God's people with abundant fruits of holiness, they sway them by their example, and they enlarge the Church by their hidden apostolic fruitfulness. They are thus an ornament to the Church and a fount of heavenly graces'' (*Perfectae Caritatis*, n. 7). Moreover, Elizabeth's doctrine, which is the fruit of her lived experience, is presented as a concrete realization of the divine vocation offered to each and every person. ''The dignity of man rests above all on the fact that he is called to communion with God. The invitation to converse with God is addressed to man as soon as he comes into being'' (*Gaudium et Spes*, n. 19).

For this reason also Father Borriello's book is very appropriate in this time of spiritual unrest and revival, of interior searching and experience. Especially for the person who is listening, it is a stimulating message and a haunting challenge to live the mystery of the Blessed Trinity in one's own spiritual temple.

The good that these pages can effect should touch countless persons, transforming their lives and giving light to their path. Elizabeth of the Trinity is a fascinating witness to the restoration of the primacy of contemplation in the Christian life, both as a spiritual itinerary and as a goal to be sought. Truly, hers was a vocation realized according to the plan of God.

† Anastasio Cardinal Ballestrero, O.C.D.

TABLE OF CONTENTS

CHRONOLOGY OF THE LIFE OF SISTER ELIZABETH

1880   Birth of Elizabeth on July 18 in Camp d'Avor, near Bourges, France, to Francis Joseph and Marie Rolland Catez. Baptized on July 22 and given the names Marie Josephine Elizabeth.

1887   The Catez family moves to Dijon and takes up residence near the monastery of Discalced Carmelite nuns. The father dies on October 2. After her first confession, Elizabeth changes her conduct radically and resolves to become a religious when she is of age.

1891   Receives First Communion on April 19. During her first visit to the Carmel of Dijon, the Prioress tells Elizabeth the name she will take as a religious and its meaning: house of God, of the Trinity.

1894   Elizabeth makes a vow of perpetual virginity and is increasingly aware of her vocation to Carmel.

1897   Reveals to her mother her desire to enter Carmel, but is refused permission.

1899   During a retreat preached by Father Cherney, S.J., in January, Elizabeth receives the first grace of prayer. In February she begins to read *The Way of Perfection* by St. Teresa of Avila. From March 4 to April 2, during the general mission preached by the Redemptorist Fathers, she experiences an intense religious fervor and an ardent zeal for souls, like the prophet Elijah. In making a general confession she is given the assurance that by divine favor she has preserved her baptismal innocence and she confirms her vocation to Carmel. On March 26 her mother assures her that she may enter Carmel when she reaches the age of 21. On March 31 she offers herself as a victim for a sinner and for the sins of the world. In June she resumes her visits to Carmel and places herself under the direction of the Prioress, Mother Mary of Jesus.

1900   In January she takes part in a retreat preached by Father Hoppenot, S.J., and resolves to live the Carmelite life in the world, prior to her entrance into Carmel. In February, during a visit with Father Vallée, O.P., she receives a satisfactory explanation of the theology of the indwelling of the Trinity and has an especially keen awareness of the Trinity dwelling in her soul.

1901   In June Mother Mary of Jesus leaves for Paray-le-Monial to establish a new Carmel. Mother Germaine of Jesus becomes Prioress at Dijon and will be in office until the death of Elizabeth. On August 2 Elizabeth enters Carmel as a postulant. She receives the habit on December 8 and is given the name Sister Elizabeth of the Trinity.

1902   In August Elizabeth begins to experience interior trials, two months after a retreat preached by Father Vallée, O.P., on the theme of the soul of Christ. In spite of his good will and theological knowledge, the Dominican Father is unable to understand Elizabeth's state of soul.

1903   Elizabeth makes her religious profession on January 11. Soon after, she experiences ineffable peace of soul and she receives the veil of a professed nun on January 21. In November she begins to read the works of St. John of the Cross.

1904   After reading the encyclical of Pope Pius X, *Omnia instaurare in Christo*, Elizabeth composes a poem on the theme of the encyclical, "to restore all things in Christ." On November 21 she is inspired to compose her famous *Elevation* to the Blessed Trinity, a synthesis of her experience and her spiritual doctrine.

1905   In the first months of the year Elizabeth experiences the symptoms of the illness that will take her to the grave. She is relieved of her duties and allowed to follow a less rigid observance of Carmelite life. At Easter she discovers her particular vocation as *Laudem gloriae* of the Trinity.

1906   On January 1, in view of her imminent death, she entrusts herself to the fatherly care of St. Joseph, Protector of the Order of Carmel. In February she is fully convinced that her personal vocation will be realized in the measure that she is conformed to the death of Christ — a reality that she is called to live in a special way in this last period of her life.

At the beginning of Lent, in reading St. Paul's letter to the Philippians 3:10, she feels that St. Paul is predicting her approaching death. After a severe crisis suffered on March 1, she is placed permanently in the infirmary. Anticipating what is yet to come, she abandons herself totally to the divine will.

On Palm Sunday, April 8, the illness reaches such a point that she receives Holy Viaticum and the Last Anointing. But on Holy Saturday she shows a sudden and unexpected improvement.

At the beginning of May she suffers a serious relapse and, in order to sustain her, the Lord grants her the grace of feeling the presence of God (May 24).

In July Elizabeth speaks at length with the Prioress, thus gaining an ever deeper understanding of her vocation to Christ crucified. In the meantime, she composes for her sister, Margaret Chevignard, a retreat entitled *How to Find Heaven on Earth*. In the latter part of August, at the explicit desire of the Prioress, she composes the *Last Retreat*.

On October 15, the feast of St. Teresa of Avila, she has her last visit with her spiritual director, Father Vallée, O.P., and with the members of her family, gathered in the parlor. The following day she was subjected to unbearable pain and was confined to bed amidst intense suffering. Towards the end of October she submitted her spiritual testament to Mother Germaine, the Prioress.

On November 1 Elizabeth received her last Communion and then entered upon an intense death agony. The community assembled for the prayers for the dying. At six o'clock in the morning, November 9, 1906, she passed sweetly and swiftly from this world to heaven, to sing the praises of the Trinity for all eternity.

1984   November 25. On the Feast of Christ the King, Elizabeth of the Trinity was beatified by Pope John Paul II.

INTRODUCTION

SOME TIME AGO, Karl Barth stated: "The Trinity of God is the mystery of his beauty. To deny it is to have a God without splendor, without joy (and without humor!), a God without beauty."[1] This statement, which is very profound and depicts well the mystery of the Trinity, is astonishing because in fact the dogma of the Trinity — one divine nature and three divine persons — the essential nucleus of the Catholic faith, has always seemed mysterious, incomprehensible, unattainable, and consequently a topic reserved for students of theology. For this reason if one wishes to discover the profundity of the trinitarian mystery and to experience the charm of its radiant beauty, one must have recourse to the sources that reveal its essence to some extent: divine revelation, the patristic teaching, the magisterium of the Church, and the experience of the mystics as well as one's own experience.

The Second Vatican Council describes the mystery of the Trinity with magisterial wisdom as a reality that can be lived by every Christian in his own interior life, because this is the vocation of every baptized person. "It pleased God, in his goodness and wisdom, to reveal himself and to make known the mystery of his will (cf. Ep 1:9). His will was that all of us should have access to the Father, through Christ, the Word made flesh, in the Holy Spirit, and thus become sharers in the divine nature (cf. Ep 2:18; 2 P 1:4). By this revelation, then, the invisible God (cf. Col 1:15; 1 Tm 1:17), from the fullness of his love, addresses each of us as his friends (cf. Ex 33:11; Jn 15:14-15), and moves among us (cf. Ba

3:38), in order to invite and receive us into his own company'' (*Dei Verbum*, n. 2). The friendly intimacy that God offers us in relation to his life and that of the three divine Persons is not something purely abstract and a matter of purely intellectual speculation; rather, it has a decidedly existential significance. The mystery in which the Father makes us sharers through baptism is the object of the gift of faith and is a gratifying possession. From this perspective the unity and trinity of God are not to be perceived in mathematical terms but as the *unity* or *unicity* and the *diversity* of a reality, because ''even if the Divinity which transcends all things is exalted as unity or as trinity, it is nevertheless neither three nor one in the sense that we conceive these things numerically.''[2]

The reality of the Trinity is a salvific and communal event: the condescending coming of the one and triune God who saves us and makes us sharers in the *koinonia* of the Trinity. It is a gratuitous manifestation of the infinite God who is love, who approaches us as Father, Son and Holy Spirit, to seize us, permeate us and elevate us to the point that we can *experience* God's own life of love. Consequently, the God of the Christian faith, who is revealed in the Son and operates in the very depth of human experience through the action of the Holy Spirit, is not a stranger to human existence; on the contrary, he is vitally involved in the intimate structure of every human being. In fact, God's revelation, beginning with creation and culminating in the recapitulation and restoration of all things in Christ, is a vital communication of himself as *agape*, as the infinite love of the Father and the Son, who mutually love one another and communicate this love to us in the Spirit of love. This fullness of life, transmitted through love and in love, stimulates an existential response to the mystery of God on our part. That response transcends all human limits and is a total giving of self to the Other, with the result that we personally experience a love that is a sharing of life with the Father in the Son through the power of the Holy Spirit. Briefly, in revealing to us the inner life of God as a mystery and as the activation of the divine fatherhood and filiation in the effusion of the Holy Spirit, Jesus, by an exigency of love, not only made known the hidden meaning of the plan of salvation, but he indicated the ultimate goal of our human vocation: called by name to share in the life of God the Father, we have been redeemed and ransomed through the blood of the only-begotten Son. In virtue of this salvific event, we have become brothers and sisters of Christ and adopted children of the one Father; and, interiorly vivified by the Holy Spirit, we become members of the divine family.

For all of these profound reasons it is not by chance that the Second Vatican Council, in the light of revelation and tradition, affirms that ''the dignity of man rests above all on the fact that he is called to communion with God. The invitation to converse with God is addressed to man as soon as he comes into being. For if man exists it is because God has created him through love, and through love continues to hold him in existence. He cannot live fully according to truth unless he freely acknowledges that love and entrusts himself to his Creator'' (*Gaudium et Spes*, n. 19). If it is true that this is our vocation (because it is the teaching of revelation, tradition and the magisterium of the Church), it is likewise true that mystics throughout the centuries have confirmed this teaching by their own personal experience.

Such is the case of Elizabeth of the Trinity, the Carmelite of Dijon, who placed the mystery of the Trinity at the very center of her spiritual life. In the stages of her spiritual journey this mystery is verified not by arid intellectual speculation but by a concrete mode of living the mystery in the ordinary events of her brief existence on earth. It is a new manner of life that can be verified by an experience that is possible for all, is attainable by all, and is for all a definite invitation. Consequently, Elizabeth of the Trinity can be considered a new prophet for our times who is an authority, not only because of her sanctity but because in living the life of a Carmelite she strove to make the mystery of the Trinity not simply an object of theological reflection but of a lived faith that permeated the very warp and woof of her existence.

As a prophet, she proclaims by her life a message of interpersonal love with the one and triune God. Her consuming love for Christ incarnate who is the way to an experiential love of the Father; her willingness to be led by the Spirit along the paths of the inscrutable mystery of the Trinity; her charism of divine intimacy within the temple of her soul; all this makes her a teacher of contemporary spirituality. The experience of her life makes her one of the exemplary models — perhaps one of the simplest, on a par with St. Therese of Lisieux — for attaining and enjoying communion of life with the divine Persons.

The divine dialogue experienced by Elizabeth in her interior life is not confined to the walls of her monastery or to a small group of consecrated souls. It has a universal resonance that can touch — and not lightly but forcefully — the interior life of any adult Christian. Persons who thirst for the absolute which is God and are attracted by the mystery of the Trinity which is attainable only in the silence of the spirit, even among the changing and distracting events of human life, will find in Elizabeth a dynamic example of how to reach union with God in the heart of the world. Indeed, the ecstatic contemplation of God does not require a flight from the events of human society, but rather a positive and incisive dedication, through one's own actions, to a world that perceives and secretly follows the interior and vital bond that unites one to God.

From this follows another characteristic that confirms the relevance of Elizabeth's message: the meaning of authentic prayer, understood as a spontaneous return to the divine, as a spiritual and religious awakening, as a continual interior renewal that is translated into moral behavior in accordance with the teaching of the Gospel. It is a spiritual journey from the external world to one's interior (*a going to one's inner room, cf. Mt 6:6*), a new and clearer knowledge of self as a partner of God who is love, an original and typical perception of and identification with one's own ego and the joyful and painful history of humanity, taken up and made one's own in order to present it to God as an object of redemption, liberation and communication with the divine being. Unlike many of the gurus who are popular today, Elizabeth reminds the busy Christian that interior silence is not a frightening void or an extreme concentration of one's own faculties; rather, it is a prayerful encounter with the living and life-giving God who communicates to us individually his merciful love and introduces us to the secrets of the life of the Trinity. Thus, Elizabeth writes:

> *The Blessed Trinity, then, is our dwelling-place, our home, our Father's house, which we should never leave... So we should descend daily by this path into the abyss, which is God himself. Let us glide into its depths with loving confidence. "Deep calleth on deep"* (Ps 41:8). *It is there, sunk to its lowest depth, that the abyss of our nothingness will find itself face to face with the abyss of the mercy, with the immensity of the All of God.*[3]

Made a sharer in the selfsame Spirit of Jesus, we are inserted into the very heart of the trinitarian mystery: "Since our Lord dwells in our souls, his prayer is ours. I wish to share in it constantly, to keep myself as a little jug at the spring, at the fountain of life, in order that I may be able subsequently to give him to souls, by permitting the waters of his charity to overflow."[4]   Thus the young Carmelite grasps the central nucleus of Christian prayer as an interpersonal and loving communion with the Trinity dwelling in the soul of the individual:

> *Prayer does not mean binding ourselves to recite a certain number of vocal prayers daily but the raising of the soul to God through all circumstances, which establishes us in a kind of continual communion with the most Holy Trinity, quite simply by doing everything in its sight... Let us enter*

*into our deepest interior, there, where the Father, the Son
and the Holy Spirit dwell, and we shall become one with
them.*[5]

So it is that Elizabeth, basing her spirituality on the teaching of
Christ, becomes a mystic who by her own experience instructs,
inspires and leads the disposed soul to intimate communion with
the Trinity in contemplative prayer.

The purpose of this little book is to confirm the relevance of
Elizabeth's message by describing in an original and personal way
the distinctive and essential elements that constitute her spiritual
make-up. The procedure is very simple; the stages are presented in
an orderly fashion in order to provide, though not definitively nor
in great detail, an overall view of the spirituality of Elizabeth of the
Trinity.

The words of the second book of Maccabees serve as a fitting
conclusion: "If it is well written and to the point, that is what I
wanted; if it is poorly done and mediocre, that is the best I could
do" (2 M 15:38). Let the reader understand that he who writes is
attempting to offer wisdom and knowledge in this book. "Happy
the man who meditates on these things; wise the man who takes
them to heart. If he puts them into practice, he can cope with
anything, for the fear of the Lord is his lamp" (Si 50:27-29).

LUIGI BORRIELLO, O.C.D.

FOOTNOTES

1 K. Barth, *Kirchliche Dogmatik*, II, pp. 1-2, Zurich, 1948-1955.
2 St. Maximus, *Commentary on the Divine Names*, 13.
3 The retreat of Sister Elizabeth, "Heaven on Earth," as quoted in M.M. Philipon, *The
   Spiritual Doctrine of Sister Elizabeth of the Trinity*, tr. by a Benedictine of Stanbrook
   Abbey, p. 220, Newman Press, Westminster, MD, 1961. Wherever possible, the
   quotations from the writings of Sister Elizabeth are taken from the work by Philipon.
4 Letter to Abbé Chevignard, December 25, 1904.
5 Letter to Mlle. G. de Gemeaux, February, 1905.

Spiritual Doctrine Of
BLESSED ELIZABETH OF THE TRINITY

APOSTOLIC CONTEMPLATIVE

CHAPTER ONE

CALLED BY NAME

BEFORE TRACING the spiritual itinerary of Elizabeth of the Trinity in order to select the essential traits of her spirituality, it will be helpful to reflect on the meaning of her name. This is not done out of idle speculation, but because her name is as it were a synthesis of the entire program of her life, from beginning to end, as it developed under the sign of the Holy Spirit. Elizabeth's progressive deepening awareness during her brief existence on earth of being called to a dialogue in faith with the triune God is contained germinally in the name she received at baptism. It signifies her being called by God; and her personal inclinations disposed her for a style of life that was in the mind of God from all eternity. Her total response, prompted by the Spirit of God, is identified with the realization of her creaturely existence. "There is no true humanism but that which is open to the Absolute and is conscious of a vocation which gives human life its true meaning."[1]

If it is true that Elizabeth finds her full realization in being open to the Absolute which is God, it is likewise true that she finds it in her life as a religious because, called to the highest peaks of intimate union with God, she responds with the gift of her entire self. "The dignity of man rests above all on the fact that he is called to communion with God. The invitation to converse with God is addressed to man as soon as he comes into being."[2]

The vocation of Elizabeth is manifested in what we have

previously called a kind of ineffable dialogue in faith, hope, and
charity between herself and God one and three, who is ever in act
and who enabled her to reach her full potential in the measure that
she was faithful to the divine promptings in the present moment of
her daily existence. "Have I ever told you my name at Carmel —
Mary Elizabeth of the Trinity? It seems to me that this name
indicates a particular vocation. Isn't it beautiful? I so love this
mystery of the Holy Trinity! It is an abyss in which I lose myself."[3]

On the feast of the Blessed Trinity in 1902 she understood more
clearly the vocation contained in her name. "This feast of the
'Three' is truly my feast. For me, there is no other like it; never
have I so well understood the mystery, and all the meaning of the
vocation expressed by my name."[4]

Known and predestined from eternity and called by name to be
Elizabeth of the Trinity, she is asked to respond in time to the plan
of God's love. That is what constitutes the supporting foundation of
the road that leads Elizabeth from baptismal anointing to mystical
union with the Trinity, enjoyed ahead of time in this life, though
only in part.

Known And Predestined From Eternity

WITH A FEW STROKES of the pen St. Paul describes the marvelous
stages of the history of salvation, overshadowed by the presence of
uncreated Love that enables one to grow and to travel along the way
of perfection: "We know that God makes all things work together
for the good of those who have been called according to his decree.
Those whom he foreknew he predestined to share the image of his
Son. . . Those he predestined he likewise called; those he called he
also justified; and those he justified he in turn glorified" (Rm
8:28-30).

According to the Pauline text and the understanding of
Elizabeth, an individual's vocation is nothing other than the fulfillment of eternal predestination or God's choice:

> *"Those whom he has foreknown." Are we not of that number? . . . Yes, we have become his through baptism, that is what Paul means by these words: "He called them"; yes, called to receive the seal of the Holy Trinity. . . Then, he has justified us by his sacraments, by his direct touches in our contemplation "in the depths" of our soul[5] . . . And finally, he wants to glorify us, . . . but we will be glorified in the measure in which we will have been conformed to the image of his divine Son.[6]*

With the passing of time the life of Elizabeth encompasses the creation of being and the elevation to grace with the predestination to become the praise of glory. Together with this itinerary there develops the mysterious and interior dialogue between God, who calls with the gratuitous love of predilection, and Elizabeth, who answers the call by the generous response of her religious consecration.

> *Such is the life of a Carmelite. She is above all a contemplative . . . and her divine life is a continuous gift of self, in an exchange of love with him who takes possession of her to the point of wanting to transform her into himself.[7]*

Meditating on predestination to filiation in the Son, she discovers the gratuitous and merciful love of God towards creatures and the vocation to which she has been called becomes ever clearer to her.

> *"God has predestined us to the adoption of children through Jesus Christ, in union with him, according to the decree of his will."[8] . . . "It is to bring us to this abyss of glory that God has created us in his image and likeness."[9]*

"See," says St. John, "what manner of love the Father has bestowed on us, that we should be called children of God; and such we are. . . Now we are the children of God, and we have not yet seen what we shall be. We know that when he appears, we shall be like him, for we shall see him just as he is. And everyone who has this hope in him makes himself holy, just as he himself is holy." [10]

Elizabeth frequently returns to the causal relationship between predestination and adoptive sonship in the context of the attainment of sanctity.

How rich we are in the gifts of God, we who are predestined to divine *adoption and we who are therefore* heirs of his heritage of glory! *"From all eternity God has chosen us in him that we might be holy in his sight in love."* [11] *Thus, we are called to that in virtue of a "divine decree," as the great apostle says.* [12]

Elizabeth's own path to sanctity takes its form and structure from this substantial nucleus. Once again, it is St. Paul, the theologian from whom the Carmelite takes her doctrine, who explains to her of what the divine election consists, when he states explicitly the heights to which Christians are called: ''God chose us in him before the world began, to be holy and blameless in his sight, to be full of love."[13] To be holy in the practice of love of God and of neighbor, this is the beginning, the middle and the end of Elizabeth's vocation.

To strive with all her strength for this sanctity, the nun of Dijon perceives that the principal task she must perform throughout her spiritual journey is *to be a praise of glory*, in conformity with the vocation received at baptism. ''*Laudem gloriae*. I have read this expression in St. Paul and I have understood that this is my vocation throughout the time of exile while awaiting the eternal

Sanctus.''[14]   A year later she returns to the same theme, describing in grand strokes the work she must undertake in order to realize her vocation.

"Nescivi.''[15]   *I no longer know anything, I do not want to know anything except ''to know* him, *to share in his sufferings, to become like him in his death.''*[16]   *''Those whom God has foreknown he has also predestined to become conformed to the image of his divine Son,''*[17]   *the One crucified by love. When I am wholly identified with this divine Exemplar, when I have wholly passed into him and he into me, then I will fulfill my eternal vocation: the one for which God ''has chosen me in him''*[18]   *''in* principio,'' *the one I will continue ''in* aeternum'' *when, immersed in the bosom of my Trinity, I will be the unceasing praise of his glory,* Laudem gloriae ejus.[19]

In a later passage she refers more explicitly to the path she has travelled in order to respond adequately to God's call: "But how do we respond to the dignity of this vocation? This is the secret: *'Mihi vivere Christus est! . . . Vivo enim, jam non ego, vivit vero in me Christus.'* [*'To me, ''life'' means Christ. . . The life I have now is not my own; Christ is living in me.'*][20]   We must be transformed into Jesus Christ.''[21]

In following Jesus, the ''divine Adorer'' and ''the praise of glory to the Father''[22] in compliance with his sufferings, Elizabeth resolves to imitate her divine Master in his constant and faithful adherence to the will of the Father. The soul of Christ — her preferred book — not only reveals to her ''all the secrets of the Father,'' as she stated in the questionnaire presented to her on her entrance into Carmel,[23]   but it gives a direction, a meaning and a content to her life as a Carmelite, all of which are expressed in the name she bears. This name, which connotes election and predestination, will attain its full significance in the hereafter, where she "will live, like the immutable Trinity, in an *eternal present*, 'adoring him always because of himself,'[24] and becoming by an always more simple, more unitive gaze, 'the splendor of his glory,'[25] that is, the unceasing praise of glory of his adorable perfections."[26]

Spiritual Journey

HAVING DISCOVERED the *leit-motif* of the life of Elizabeth, we can accompany her on the spiritual itinerary that leads her, with Christ and the Virgin Mary, to intimate union with the three divine Persons. Choleric, impulsive and vivacious from early infancy, she manifests an indomitable will and a strong character, but sensitive to the point of being able to penetrate to the heart of things. Patient and at the same time always available, divine grace effected in her a notable change at the time of her first confession and First Communion. This first direct and personal encounter with God aroused in her a profound sense of the divine and orientated her in a definitive manner toward the Absolute.

My soul became his dwelling-place, his property, his kingdom, and from that day, from that mysterious and holy colloquium, I thought only of giving him my life, of making some small return for the great love of my Beloved in the Eucharist.[27]

Innundated with sanctifying grace, Elizabeth was radically changed and she pledged herself to be governed henceforth by love.[28]

It seems that on the very afternoon of her First Communion day, Elizabeth was brought to the Carmel of Dijon and the Prioress, who knew her name, explained its meaning: "House of God." The explanation made a deep impression on the child and from that moment on, she knew how to live in intimate union with the living

God present within her. In fact, in later years, even when in the midst of distractions and mundane festivities, she always preserved a special attention to the divine Guest in her soul. As she herself wrote later: ''I belonged entirely to God. In the midst of parties and social gatherings I was so taken up with my Master and the thought of receiving Communion on the following day that I became insensible and far removed from what was going on around me.''[29]

Still feeling the need for a theological explanation of the name she bore, she was never satisfied with any other explanation than the one given by the Dominican, Father Vallée, at the Carmel of Dijon. Little Elizabeth listened with attention and joy to the words of the Dominican Father as he commented on the words: ''Are you not aware that you are the temple of God, and that the Spirit of God dwells in you?'' (1 Cor 3:16). She thus obtained an understanding of the great love of God (Ep 2:4) by which she allowed herself to be captivated.

It seems to me that nothing can distract one from him when one acts only for him, always in his holy presence, under that divine glance that penetrates to the depths of the soul. Even in the midst of the world it is possible to listen to him in the silence of a heart that wants to be his alone.[30]

Her deep union with God was affirmed yet another time when she wrote: ''This presence of God is so beautiful! It is in the very depths of my being, in the heaven of my soul that I love to find him so that he will never abandon me. 'God in me; I in him.' He is my whole life.''[31] This is the secret of her life before she entered Carmel; this is the mystery of love that sustained her throughout her religious life within the walls of the cloister.

Before completing her fourteenth year, Elizabeth consecrated herself to Jesus and the Blessed Virgin by a vow of virginity. She renewed this consecration on every Marian feast in order to manifest her total availability to God's action within her. Around the age of fourteen, during thanksgiving after Communion, she experienced a strong attraction for Carmel. From that moment on, she exerted every effort to enter Carmel as soon as possible, in order to fulfill her desire for communion with God, "the heritage that Elijah left to the sons of Carmel."[32]   Indeed, her union with God was the mainstay of her entire life on earth.

After receiving her mother's permission, Elizabeth entered Carmel on August 2, 1901, and was given the religious name, Mary Elizabeth of the Trinity. Determined and tenacious in the pursuit of her goal, she resolved to live up to her name (House of God), as is evident from the response she gave in the questionnaire that she filled out when she entered Carmel: "God in me and I in him." She chose this phrase as her motto and she would live it by being ever present to God within her through a life of love and continual immolation. In fact, soon after entering Carmel she wrote to her sister Marguerite: "Everything is delightful in Carmel. One finds the good God in the laundry as well as in prayer. In every place there is nothing but God. One lives and breathes him everywhere."[33]

Elizabeth's constant effort to tend toward the goal she had proposed for herself and to be completely open to the action of the divine presence oriented her life decisively toward the very sanctity of God. Mother Germaine of Jesus stated in a deposition: "In my opinion the characteristic of this life, hidden in God, truly consists in Elizabeth's special fidelity in heroically living her faith in the presence of God, or rather in God, in the depth of her soul. That was her sanctification or, if I dare say so, her martyrdom."[34] Besides, she had gone to Carmel to become a saint for the Church and for the glory of God.[35]   She found the basic elements of sanctity in the Carmelite Rule which permeated her religious life. As she said: "I love this Rule which is the manner in which he wants me to be holy."[36]   And God wanted her to be holy not in any theoretical manner but very concretely, offering himself as a model of life and the measure of perfection. Thus, Elizabeth writes:

> *To be holy as God is holy, such is, it seems, the measure of the children of his love! Did not the Master say: "Be perfect as your heavenly Father is perfect"?*[37]

> *This is the measure of the holiness of the children of God: "to be holy as God, to be holy with the holiness of God"; and we do this by living close to him in the depths of the bottomless abyss "within." "Then the soul seems in some way to resemble God."*[38]

In her prayer, in her daily work, in her availability, open and generous with the other nuns, in silence and obscurity, as a good contemplative and a true daughter of St. John of the Cross, Elizabeth knew that to attain to the holiness of God she had to conform herself in all things to Christ, the revelation of the Father. "Then I will have wholly passed into him and can say: 'I no longer live. My Master lives in me.' And I will be '*holy, pure, without reproach*' in the Father's eyes."[39] With good reason, therefore, could a fellow religious give the following testimony years later: "What was especially evident in her in the three years following her profession was her fidelity in burying herself in silence in order to live hidden with Christ in God, according to the Pauline phrase that was so dear to her."[40]

Not only that, but Elizabeth knew that in order to attain the desired sanctity she must die with and in Christ crucified. "To share in the sufferings of my crucified Spouse and to walk with him to meet my suffering, to be a redemptrix with him. St. Paul says that *those whom God has foreknown, he has predestined to be conformed to the image of his Son.* Rejoice in your maternal heart that God has predestined me and has signed me with the seal of the cross of his Christ."[41]

Elizabeth did not in any way refuse to walk that path. For her the cross was not a point of departure; it was a familiar path along which she advanced voluntarily in order to share in anticipation the eternal glory of the blessed. To share in the sufferings of Christ by means of her bodily pains meant for her that she was a good way along the path that leads to *the glorious mystery of the sanctity of the Three*. In the last months of her life, when the illness had become acute, she accepted with great faith the dreadful martyrdom of her atrocious sufferings. During one of the periods of her most intense pain she wrote: "I am tasting, experiencing joys hitherto unknown: the joy of suffering. . . *Before I die it is my dream to be transformed into Jesus crucified*, and this is what gives me such fortitude in suffering."[42]   In the last days of her extreme suffering Elizabeth began to understand fully the hidden meaning of her name in the context of the vocation of Carmel: *Praise of glory*.

> *"For whom he foreknew," St. Paul tells us, "He also predestined to be made conformable to the image of his Son." That is what I am going to teach myself: conformity, identity with my adored Master who was crucified for love! Then I shall be able to fulfill my office of Praise of Glory and even here below to sing the eternal Sanctus, while waiting to go and chant it in the heavenly courts of the Father's house.*[43]

Docile under the hands of the Holy Spirit, with incomparable generosity and courage, she let him engrave on her flesh his sanctifying imprint. By the power of unifying and transfiguring grace she thus became like unto Christ crucified in all things.

> *St. Paul gives me light on this when he writes to his followers his wish that "the Father would strengthen them inwardly with power through his Spirit so that Christ would dwell*

through faith in their hearts, and so that they would be rooted and grounded in love."[44] *To be rooted and grounded in love: such, it seems to me, is the condition for worthily fulfilling its work as praise of glory. The soul that penetrates and dwells in these "depths of God" of which the royal prophet sings, and thus does everything "in him, with him, by him and for him" with that limpid gaze which gives it a certain resemblance to the simple Being, this soul, by each of its movements, its aspirations, as well as by each of its acts, however ordinary they may be, "is rooted" more deeply in him whom it loves. Everything within it pays homage to the thrice-holy God: it is so to speak a perpetual Sanctus, an unceasing praise of glory!*[45]

The life of Elizabeth is an ascetico-mystical hymn composed on the bed of the most painful suffering. It is a hymn sung in the silence of her heart, already united with her divine Spouse under the divine touch of the Spirit of love. Earlier she had written: "A praise of glory is a soul of silence that remains like a lyre under the mysterious touch of the Holy Spirit so that he may draw from it divine harmonies; it knows that suffering is a string that produces still more beautiful sounds; so it loves to see this string on its instrument that it may more delightfully move the Heart of its God."[46]   A praise of glory offers herself completely as a *victim of praise* to the fire that is consuming her life of oblation. Now, nearing the end of her strength and suffering intensely, Elizabeth realizes the intimate union with the Trinity which she had described in her prayer to the Blessed Trinity, composed in 1904:

O my God, Trinity whom I adore, help me to forget myself entirely that I may be established in you as still and as peaceful as if my soul were already in eternity. May nothing trouble my peace or make me leave you, O my unchanging One, but may each minute carry me further into the depths of your mystery. Give peace to my soul; make it your heaven, your beloved dwelling and your resting place. May I never leave you there alone but be wholly present, my faith wholly vigilant, wholly adoring, and wholly surrendered to your creative action.[47]

Alone on her Calvary, nailed to the cross of suffering, after a violent crisis she asks the Lord, Fire of Love, to consume her little by little for his glory and for the extension of the kingdom of God. Before leaving this world she is vividly aware of the presence of the Blessed Virgin, her favorite model, who for the last time takes her by the hand to escort her definitively into the mystery of her Three. With a smile on her lips and as a conclusion to her earthly life of praise and glory of the Trinity, she murmured her last words: "I am going to Light, to Love, to Life."[48]

Having completed her spiritual journey on earth, Elizabeth continues her mission from heaven, as she had promised: "It seems to me that in heaven my mission will be to draw souls, by helping them to go out of themselves in order to adhere to God by a very simple, wholly loving movement and to maintain them in that great inner silence which allows God to imprint himself on them and to transform them into himself."[49]

Between The Now And The Not Yet

IN ELIZABETH'S VIEW, to place herself within the divine plan for her required first of all a total response in faith to the gratuitous invitation of God until she had fully done his will in joy. "How beautiful it is to unite, to identify our will with his! Then we shall be always happy, always content."[50]   To this end she humbly prayed: "that I may be faithful, that I may penetrate in depth his plans for my soul, that I may do his will perfectly."[51]   Actually, behind this prayer was hidden her desire for sanctity, which was so very evident in her life as a dominating force.

"Be holy because I am holy." These words are the motto of my retreat. They are the light in whose rays I shall walk during my divine journey. St. Paul supplies the commentary when he says: "God chose us in [Christ] before the world began, to be holy and blameless in his sight, to be full of love."[52]

For Elizabeth, communion with God is not something unattainable. In fact "to abide in God" — an expression often used by her — does not imply something static, but dynamic. It signifies constant progress in faith, hope and charity toward mystical union with the Three. When she speaks of walking in the presence of God, she means a joyful and constant movement, not on the limited human level, but on that of the eternal already begun, because it is permeated with the creative touch of God who is present in all things.

Speaking to Abraham, God said: "Walk in my presence and be perfect." This then is the way to achieve this perfection that our heavenly Father asks of us! St. Paul, after having immersed himself in the divine counsels, revealed exactly this to us when he wrote: "God has chosen us in him before the creation of the world, that we might be holy and immaculate in his presence in love." It is also by the light of this same saint that I will be enlightened so that I might walk without deviating from this magnificent road of the presence of God on which the soul journeys "alone with the Alone."[53]

In order to put into practice the invitation and the plan of God, Elizabeth followed as perfectly as possible the person of Christ, who in himself provides an entire program of life. With the incarnation of Christ, the seat of the word of God, the transcendent is no longer heaven but the life of charity in and with Christ, from whom nothing can ever separate her. She writes along these lines to a friend:

> *Let him complete in you the work of predestination, and to do this, heed the words of St. Paul: "Continue, therefore, to live in Christ Jesus the Lord, in the spirit in which you received him. Be rooted in him and built up in him, growing ever stronger in faith, as you were taught, and overflowing with gratitude."*[54] *Be rooted in him, and therefore detached from self.*[55]

In another letter she writes in the same vein: "Of ourselves we are nothingness and sin, but he is the Holy One and he dwells within us in order to save us, to purify us and to transform us into himself. Remember the beautiful challenge of the Apostle: 'Who will separate me from the charity of Christ?' It is in following Christ and especially in letting herself be acted upon and led by his Spirit of love that Elizabeth will succeed in living heaven upon earth."[56]

Her prompt and total response, her unconditional consent to God's invitation, her complete adhesion to the will of the Beloved in Carmel are all phases of a marvelous adventure in Carmel that enabled her to enter, together with Christ, docile, obedient and faithful to the will of the Father, the threshold of eternal life even in this world. She said as much in a letter to her sister: "If you only knew how beautiful this Carmel is, this 'alone with the Alone,' with him who is loved! Yes, it is an anticipated heaven; don't be envious, my dear!"[57]   In another letter, she writes: "When you think of your little Carmelite, give thanks to him who has reserved such a beautiful portion for her. Sometimes I think that it is a foretaste of heaven."[58]

If Elizabeth was able to describe her life in Carmel as an "anticipated heaven," it was because she had broken every bond to the world and to herself by means of her religious profession.

Not only that, but to be faithful to her commitment and to live joyfully the radical choice she had made, transcending self and the things of this world, she had to die to self each day. "If you were to ask me the secret of happiness," she wrote, "I would say that it consists in taking no account whatever of self and in practicing self-denial at every moment."[59]

To experience in the present moment a sampling of intimate union with the triune God while waiting for the veil to be removed so that she could fully enjoy her Three, this constitutes, as it were, the two extreme poles of her life on earth: her existential response to the invitation to union with God, having as a point of departure her election by God and as a logical development the faithful and consistent effort to live joyfully with, through and in Christ Jesus. "Happily, after this exile we shall be able to live in him! Therefore the happiness of my Master suffices to make me happy and I surrender myself to him so that he can do in me whatever he wishes."[60]

Ushered into the divine sphere even in this life, Elizabeth was able to see all things from another viewpoint, in their very essence. Thus, she wrote to her doctor: "In this last hour of my exile, in this beautiful evening of my life, the importance of everything is perceived by me in the light that comes from eternity. I would like to cry out to all souls and tell them the vanity, the nothingness of everything that passes away without being done for God."[61]

In this halo of light and of grace the partial understanding of the divine mystery does not overwhelm Elizabeth or fill her with fear because of its transcendence; rather, it gives her a sense of trusting cooperation with the divine life that floods her soul. "Ask him that I may always be faithful to my lofty vocation and that I will not misuse the grace he showers upon me. If you only knew how it sometimes frightens me. At such times I can only cast myself in the arms of him whom John calls 'the Faithful One' and 'the Truth,' asking that he himself be my fidelity."[62]

The Carmelite of Dijon lived her "not yet" by following the

example of the Blessed Virgin, walking in her footsteps in realizing her vocation to divine intimacy. But rather than a waiting for the blessed event, Elizabeth's life was a straining toward the full realization of her particular charism in the mystical body of Christ. ''I love to contemplate my vocation as a Carmelite in this twofold calling: 'Virgin-Mother.' Virgin, espoused to Christ in faith. Mother, saving souls, multiplying the adoptive children of the Father, co-heirs with Jesus Christ.''[63] In this immense sea of light, a preview of what she will see hereafter, the heart of Elizabeth expands to embrace all her children and brethren as a bride and a mother. At the end of her life the fervent nun has understood that the mystery of love that she lives interiorly touches the farthest limits of the world and reaches to the most hidden depths of the human heart in order to transform it and make it Christian.

At present I am reading some beautiful pages in our Holy Father, St. John of the Cross, on the transformation of the soul into the three divine Persons. To what heights of glory we are called! Oh, I quite understand the silence and the recollection of the saints, who could not emerge from their contemplation! In that state God could lead them to the divine heights where oneness is achieved between him and the soul that has become his spouse in the mystical sense of the word. Our blessed Father says that the Holy Spirit then raises it to such heights that he makes it capable of producing in God the same spiration of love that the Father produces in the Son and the Son in the Father, the spiration which is none other than the Holy Spirit himself. To think that God calls us, in virtue of our vocation, to live in this sacred splendor! What an adorable mystery of love! I want to correspond to it by living on earth as our Lady did, who "kept all these words in her heart"; I want, so to speak, to bury myself in the depths of my soul, there to lose myself in

*the Trinity which dwells there in order to transform me into
Itself. Then my motto, "my shining ideal," will be realized:
I shall truly be Elizabeth of the Trinity.*[64]

Elizabeth's desire became a reality even in this life when,
following the example of the Virgin Mary, she hid herself in the
bosom of the Trinity dwelling within her. This she did, not to
remain in ecstasy before the divine beauty, but to realize the full
meaning of her name: *house of God*. Like the Blessed Virgin,
fixing her attention on her own interior, she perceives the divine
life there and strives to penetrate ever more profoundly into herself
in order to live that life in all its depth in the sanctuary of her heart.
That is what constitutes Elizabeth's vocation; it is the secret of her
holiness, which was in turn the full realization of her name, the
name that gave the orientation to her life and her spiritual typology.
She remained ever faithful to this "intimacy with the Three," so
that shortly before her death she could say that "It has been the
beautiful Sun that irradiated my life, making it an anticipated
heaven."[65]

_____ FOOTNOTES _____

1 *Populorum Progressio*, no. 42.
2 *Gaudium et Spes*, no. 19.
3 Letter to Canon Angles, June, 1901.
4 Letter to her sister, June, 1902.
5 A reference to St. John of the Cross, *Spiritual Canticle*, Stanza 19, no. 5.
6 *Elizabeth of the Trinity: Complete Works*, Vol. I, tr. A. Kane, O.C.D., I.C.S. Publications, Washington, D.C., 1984, p. 105. Hereafter designated as *Complete Works*.
7 Letter to G. de Gemeaux, May, 1903.
8 Ep 1:5.
9 St. John of the Cross, *Spiritual Canticle*, Stanza 39, no. 4.
10 I John 3:1-3; cf. *Complete Works*, p. 107.
11 Ep 1:4.
12 Letter to F. de Sourdon, August, 1905.
13 Ep 1:4.
14 Letter to Abbé Chevignard, December, 1905.
15 From the Song of Songs, 6:1 and also cited by St. John of the Cross in *Spiritual Canticle*, Stanza 26, no. 14.
16 Ph 3:10.
17 Rm 8:29.
18 Cf. Ep 1:4.
19 *Complete Works*, p. 141.
20 Ph 1:21 and Gal 2:20.
21 *Complete Works*, p. 159.
22 Cf. M.M. Philipon, *The Spiritual Doctrine of Sister Elizabeth of the Trinity*, tr. by a Benedictine of Stanbrook Abbey, Newman Press, Wesminster, MD, 1961.
23 *Ibid.*, p. 159.
24 *Ibid.*, pp. 13-14.
25 Cf. Ps 71:15.
26 Cf. Heb 1:3.
27 *Complete Works*, p. 162.
28 From a poem composed by Elizabeth in April, 1898, on the anniversary of her First Holy Communion.
29 Recorded in Elizabeth's diary, January 30, 1899.
30 Recorded in *Summarium super virtutibus*, Postulazione dei Carmelitani Scalzi, Rome, 1967, p. 425; cf. also p. 17.
31 Letter to Canon Angles, December, 1900.
32 Letter to Canon Angles, June, 1901.
33 Letter to G. de Gemeaux, September, 1902.
34 Letter to her sister, August, 1901.
35 *Summarium super virtutibus*, p. 41, paragraph 76.
36 Cf. her letter to G. de Gemeaux, August 20, 1903, and her diary for January 23, 1900.
37 Letter to Canon Angles, July, 1903. Cf. Mt 5:48.
38 *Complete Works*, p. 151.
39 *Ibid.*, pp. 107-108.
40 *Ibid.*, p. 156.
41 *Summarium super virtutibus*, p. 77, paragraph 169. Cf. Rm 8:29.
42 Letter to her mother, July, 1906.

43 Letter to G. de Gemeaux, October, 1906. Cf. Rm. 8:29.
44 Ep 3:16-17.
45 Letter to Sister Agnes, August, 1906.
46 *Complete Works*, p. 150.
47 *Ibid.*, p. 112.
48 *Ibid.*, p. 183.
49 *Summarium super virtutibus*, p. 442.
50 Letter to Sister Marie-Odile, October, 1906, quoted by M.M. Philipon, *op. cit.*, p. 206.
51 Letter to M. Gallot, April, 1901.
52 Letter to G. de Gemeaux, May, 1906. Cf. Ep 1:4.
53 Letter to Abbé Chevignard, October, 1905.
54 Col 2:6-7.
55 *Complete Works*, p. 152.
56 Letter to F. de Sourdon, October, 1906.
57 Letter to her sister, February or March, 1902.
58 Letter to G. de Gemeaux, February, 1905.
59 Letter to Canon Angles, April, 1902.
60 Letter to F. de Sourdon, October, 1906.
61 Letter to Canon Angles, May, 1906.
62 Letter to Dr. Barbier, November, 1906.
63 Letter to Abbé Chevignard, October, 1905.
64 Letter to Abbé Chevignard, April, 1904.
65 Letter to Abbé Chevignard, November, 1903.

CHAPTER   TWO

LIKE MARY, CONTEMPLATIVE VIRGIN

IN STRIVING for full union with God, Elizabeth found in the Virgin
Mary a vivid example of fidelity to the Divine Word and docility to
the action of the Holy Spirit. She especially saw in Mary a sweet
companion on the road to the possession of the ineffable mystery of
the three Divine Persons. With complete docility she entrusted
herself to Mary, Mother of God and Mother of mankind, under the
title of Co-redemptrix.

Through sanctifying grace, by her faithful listening to the
Word, and particularly because of her intimate sharing in the
mystery of the Incarnation, the Blessed Virgin very quickly enjoyed mystical union with the Divine Persons. Closely united with
the one and triune God in a relationship of mutual love, she passed
her life absorbed in contemplation. Her silence, however, was not
one of indifferent apathy but it was at once receptivity, listening,
assent and adoration of the Word made flesh. By virtue of this
hidden solidarity with the salvific mystery, she actively
participated in everything and through everything at every moment
for the realization of God's loving plan for mankind.

Besides being a model of the contemplative life, the Blessed
Virgin is the way, together with Christ, for reaching more quickly
the mystery of the Father's love which was revealed in Christ
through the salvific power of the Holy Spirit. Joined in a special
way to Christ by the divine will, it was granted to Mary to know the

plan of the Trinity in its multiple facets and to experience it day by day in the depths of her heart as Mother of the living.

Finally, the Virgin Mary represented for Elizabeth the paradigm of apostolic activity in the mystical body, blending contemplation and action in authentic prayer without favoring one over the other, so that these alternating activities were expressions of the one and the same love in her heart. For anyone who experiences God in prayer as Mary did, contemplation is not an activity reserved for a few, while action is the lot of the majority. Contemplation and action are so united in the Blessed Virgin that they constitute but one exemplary reality for anyone who, like her, is able to be present to the world with all its problems by the simple fact of being possessed completely by God. Thus, commenting on Mary's visit to her cousin Elizabeth, the Carmelite of Dijon writes:

It seems to me that the attitude of the Virgin during the months that elapsed between the Annunciation and the Nativity is the model for interior souls, those whom God has chosen to live within, in the depths of the bottomless abyss. In what peace, in what recollection Mary lent herself to everything she did! How even the most trivial things were divinized by her! For through it all the Virgin remained the adorer of the gift of God! This did not prevent her from spending herself outwardly when it was a matter of charity; the Gospel tells us that Mary went in haste to the mountains of Judea to visit her cousin Elizabeth. Never did the ineffable vision that she contemplated within herself in any way diminish her outward charity. For, a pious author says, if contemplation "continues towards praise and towards the eternity of its Lord, it possesses unity and will not lose it. If an order from heaven arrives, contemplation turns towards men, sympathizes with their needs, is inclined towards all their miseries; it must cry and be fruitful. It illuminates like fire, and like it, it burns, absorbs and devours, lifting up to heaven what it has devoured. And when it has finished its work here below, it rises, burning with its fire, and takes up again the road on high.'' [1]

Elizabeth did not measure devotion to the Blessed Virgin by intense feeling, lest it be reduced completely to a sentimental pietism. Yet her attachment to Mary was a constant stimulus to see in the Blessed Virgin the perfect realization of her own vocation and her ideal as a contemplative Carmelite. Consequently, in the evening of her life she wanted to be consecrated anew to the Virgin Mary. "It is she, the Immaculate, who gave me the habit of Carmel, and I am asking her to clothe me anew in that robe of fine linen in which the bride is decked to present herself at the marriage feast of the Lamb."[2]   And so it was; the Blessed Virgin not only protected her during her life but she also gifted her with the titles of mother and spouse, sister and companion in her encounter with God.

Virgin Of Silence And Recollection

TO LIVE CONSTANTLY in the presence of God in purity and holiness of life required of the young Carmelite silent availability and fruitful dedication, like Mary, totally intent on listening to the Word and meditating on it in order to live it in the present moment. St. Peter Chrysologus has beautifully described the process of assimilation effected in the Christian by the Word of God:

As the text says, the kingdom of God is like a grain of mustard seed, because the kingdom is brought by a word from heaven, is received through hearing, is sown by faith, takes root through belief, grows by hope, is diffused by profession, expands through virtue, and is spread out into branches. To these branches it invites the birds of heaven,

that is, the powers of spiritual insight. In those branches it
receives them in a peaceful abode.[3]

This text, together with many others from Sacred Scripture, describes the best dispositions for receiving the Word before living it. The fruitfulness of the Word depends on a virginal disposition and an abandonment of the soul that trusts in the Word, and this calls for an atmosphere of silence and recollection. For this, we have the example of the Blessed Virgin, who "kept all these things in her heart" (Lk 2:19). Elizabeth comments on this text as follows:

"The Virgin kept all these things in her heart"; her whole
history can be summed up in these few words. It was within
her heart that she lived, and at such a depth that no human
eye can follow her.[4]

Deeply immersed in the silence of the Word, the Word made flesh, Elizabeth implicitly asks the Virgin Mary to give her her very own sentiments so that she can be an echo of the eternal Word:

Mary was always "pure, immaculate, and without reproach" *in the eyes of the thrice-holy God. Her soul is so*
simple. Its movements are so profound that they cannot be
detected. She seems to reproduce on earth the life which is
that of the divine Being, the simple Being. And she is so
transparent, so luminous that one would mistake her for the
light, yet she is but the "mirror" of the Sun of Justice:
"Speculum justitiae"![5]

In Elizabeth's vocabulary, purity, virginity and humility are the ideal dispositions of soul that enable the divine Word to take root, to grow, and to produce the desired fruit.

Called to live in the atmosphere of the mystery of the Trinity, the young religious responds with the words of the Blessed Virgin Mary: "Behold the handmaid of the Lord."

> *Like Him, her prayer was always this: "Ecce, here I am!"*
> *Who? "The servant of the Lord," the lowliest of His crea-*
> *tures: she, His Mother! Her humility was so real for she was*
> *always forgetful, unaware, freed from self.*[6]

In responding thus, Elizabeth finds herself before the infinite will of God, manifested in his Word. The encounter with the Infinite and Eternal did not frighten her but created the setting for a marvelous dialogue of love. In fact, shortly after entering Carmel, she wrote that the Carmelite "hungers for silence in order to be always listening, to penetrate ever more deeply into His infinite being."[7] Silence, solitude, recollection and adoration are all indispensable conditions for maintaining her constant union with her Three, following the example of the Blessed Virgin:

> *Do we think what must have been in the soul of the Blessed*
> *Virgin when, after the Incarnation, she possessed within her*
> *the Incarnate Word, the gift of God? In what silence, what*
> *recollection she must have buried herself in the depths of her*
> *soul in order to embrace that God whose mother she was.*[8]

Called to live the infinite Word in her interior, she learned from on high the secret of being ever more open and more receptive of divine love, thus achieving that sense of Carmelite maternity which was so evident in her spiritual life. Her close theological union with Mary, second only to her union with Christ, the great Praise of Glory of the Trinity, enabled her to exercise her new mission of spiritual motherhood, a mission that flowed from her participation in the mystery of the Trinity. In fact, she saw in the Blessed Virgin the concrete ideal of her relations to the divine Trinity and her sharing in the mission of co-redemptrix. For that reason she could with good reason write to a friend in a moment of sadness:

> *I come to you through the transpierced Heart of the Mother of Sorrows. . . Every soul that is cast into suffering lives at the side of her who shared with Jesus Christ the immensity of sorrow of which the prophet spoke. That is the dwelling-place of the predestined, of those whom the Father has known and wishes to be conformed to the image of his divine Son, the Crucified.*[9]

Through Mary and like Mary the humble Carmelite becomes a mediator of grace together with Christ crucified. Such is the grain of mustard seed described by St. Peter Chrysologus. It is sown in the virginal field that is Mary and becomes the tree of the Cross that produces a salvific fruit that is offered to the entire world. And Mary at the foot of the Cross is "the priestly Virgin whom the priest ought to contemplate and invoke constantly."[10] She is the perfect model and living example of intimate union with God.

> *It seems to me that the attitude of the Virgin during the months that elapsed between the Annunciation and the Nativity is the model for interior souls, those whom God has chosen to live within, in the depths of the bottomless abyss.*[11]

Mary is for Elizabeth the measure of her striving, the luminous figure on which she gazed in order to live her religious life, understood as meditation on and assimilation of the divine Word. She is the living incarnation of a loving faith and she seeks to conform to herself the soul that contemplates the divine source in order to transmit to her and through her to the entire world the beneficent graces of salvation.

Through Mary To The Trinity

ON THE FEAST of the Assumption in 1894 Elizabeth prayed to the Madonna in a poem: "I desire to live a hidden life, together with your Son, sweet Mother; hidden forever in your Carmel." Two days later, she addressed St. Teresa of Avila: "My Carmelite sister, beloved by Jesus, grant that he will hear my prayers also." To live hidden with Christ in God, a constant petition in her prayers, did not mean for Elizabeth to enclose herself in the little world of the cloister, but through the mediation of Christ and under the guidance of the Blessed Virgin Mary to penetrate the mystery of the Father's love through the power of the Holy Spirit.

"No one has seen the Father," says St. John, "except the Son and those to whom the Son has willed to reveal Him." It seems to me that we can also say, "No one has penetrated the depths of the mystery of Christ except the Blessed Virgin." [12]

From this springs her prayerful invitation to chosen souls: "Let us draw near to the pure and radiant Virgin, that she may lead us to Him whose mystery she has so deeply penetrated. May our life be a continual communion, a perfectly simple movement towards God." [13] Our Carmelite, who made the indwelling of the Trinity in her soul the basis of her spiritual life, finds in Mary the key to living that mystery to the full. With the help of divine grace she understood that Mary, after her decisive *fiat*, lived in intimate, silent and permanent union with the Son of God made man. Consequently, to live in the triune God signified for Elizabeth to live the mystery of the Word in and with Mary, following the movements of the Holy Spirit.

In an atmosphere of silent adoration and with all the love of which she was capable, Elizabeth constantly asked of the heavenly Mother the secret of divine intimacy.

*On the fifteenth I entrusted my desires to the Blessed Virgin.
I have asked her that in ascending to heaven she should
obtain from the treasury of the good God whatever is best for
my mamma. I also asked her to reveal to you the secret of
union with the good God that will enable you to remain
united with him throughout all events. It is the intimacy of a
baby with its mamma, of a bridegroom with the bride. Such
is the life of a Carmelite.*[14]

Besides introducing the soul to intimacy with the eternal Word, it is
the mission of the Blessed Virgin to form the chosen soul into the
image and likeness of Christ so that it may be an irradiation of his
glory and his living voice among human beings. Thus, Elizabeth
states: "This Mother of grace will form my soul so that her little
child will be a living, 'striking' image of her first-born, the Son of
the Eternal, he who was the perfect praise of his Father's
glory."[15]   Not only that, but the request that Elizabeth directs to
her heavenly Mother is the grace of being able, like her, to bring
forth so many other Christs for the Church in order to glorify the
Father in his creatures and to continue the mission of Christ the
Lord in her daily life. But to achieve this goal, Elizabeth realized
that she should associate herself with the Blessed Virgin in her role
of suffering for the redemption of mankind:

*Oh! How beautiful she is to contemplate during her long
martyrdom, so serene, enveloped in a kind of majesty that
radiates both strength and gentleness. . . She is there at the
foot of the Cross, standing, full of strength and courage, and
here my Master says to me: "Behold your mother." He
gives her to me for my Mother. . . And now that He has
returned to the Father and has substituted me for Himself on
the Cross so that "I may suffer in my body what is lacking in
His Passion for the sake of His body, which is the Church,"
the Blessed Virgin is again there to teach me to suffer as He*

did. . . when I shall have said my "consummatum est,"
[" it is finished,"] it is again she, "Janua coeli," who will
lead me into the heavenly courts.[16]

Mary, the companion of Elizabeth in her journey through life,
continues to be that in heaven at the explicit request of the young
Carmelite. She is the door and the threshold of heaven not only for
Elizabeth but for all the souls devoted to her, so that through her
they are plunged into the mystery of the eternal and blessed Trinity.
Mary's intimate relationship with the Blessed Trinity was force-
fully brought home to Elizabeth as she meditated on a picture of
Our Lady of the Incarnation, which someone had given her:

> *In the solitude of our cell, which I call my little paradise —*
> *for it is full of Him who lives in heaven — I shall often look at*
> *the precious picture, and I shall unite myself to the soul of the*
> *Blessed Virgin when the Father overshadowed her with his*
> *power, while the Word became incarnate within her, and the*
> *Holy Ghost came upon her to work the great mystery. It is*
> *the whole Trinity in action, God yielding, giving himself.*
> *And ought not the life of the Carmelite be lived under this*
> *divine action?*[17]

Recollected interiorly, Elizabeth, together with the Virgin Mary,
contemplates the mystery of the triune God, and now in the eternal
ecstasy of the beatific vision she continues to be the praise and
glory of the Trinity, as her name indicates.

Contemplative In Action

PRECISELY BECAUSE Elizabeth was deeply anchored in God, she
realized that her life of love could not be confined to the four walls
of Carmel, but that it had to embrace the joys and anxieties of all
creatures. She saw the apostolate as flowing from one's intimate

union with God: "What a great influence an apostle can exert on
souls when he remains ever united to the source of the living
waters!"[18]   The apostle who is intimately united with the divine
source can draw forth the living water to pour it out on those around
him, without ever exhausting his own supply. In this same vein
Elizabeth once wrote to a priest acquaintance:

> St. Paul says that we ''are no more strangers and foreigners
> but fellow citizens with the saints and the domestics of God.''
> We already live in the supernatural world by faith. . . In his
> magnificent Epistles, the sole theme of St. Paul's preaching
> is this mystery of the charity of Christ. . . "That Christ may
> dwell by faith in your hearts: that being rooted and founded
> in charity, you may be able to comprehend, with all the
> saints, what is the breadth and length, and height, and
> depth. To know also the charity of Christ which surpasses all
> knowledge, that you may be filled to all the fullness of God.''
> Since our Lord dwells in our souls, his prayer is ours. I wish
> to share in it constantly, to keep myself as a little jug at the
> spring, at the fountain of life, in order that I may be able
> subsequently to give him to souls, by permitting the waters of
> his charity to overflow.[19]

But Elizabeth realized that to be carried on the wings of the divine
eagle to the transcendental sphere of God, she must pass beyond
the veil of all created things. This calls for self-sacrifice and the
renunciation of all that is not God; then one can gather all others
together in prayer, especially in mental prayer, "in that intimate
heart-to-heart encounter in which the soul pours itself entirely into
God and God into it in order that he may transform it into another
self."[20]

With Mary as her companion she was led along the paths of
contemplation, "that grade of prayer in which God does everything and we do nothing, in which he unites our soul so intimately

to himself that it is no longer we who live but Jesus lives in us.''[21] As a result of this contemplative union, she was able to perceive and understand in a single glance the reality of things in their very roots. For Elizabeth contemplation meant a loving intuition that penetrates to the core of global reality because the soul is firmly rooted in Christ, the incarnate Word. As she put it: ''Every moment has been given to us that we may be more deeply 'rooted' in God, as St. Paul says, in order that our likeness to our divine model may be more amazing and our union with him more intimate.''[22] But to reach such a state Elizabeth realized that she had to detach herself from self, deny herself, and die to her own self-love.

To walk in Jesus Christ *seems to me to mean to leave self, lose sight of self, give up self, in order to enter more deeply into him with every passing moment, so deeply that one is* rooted *there; and to every event, to every circumstance we can fling this beautiful challenge: ''Who will separate me from the love of Jesus Christ?'' When the soul is established in him at such depths that its* roots *are also deeply thrust in, then the divine sap streams into it and all this imperfect, commonplace, natural life is destroyed. The soul thus ''stripped'' of self and ''clothed'' in Jesus Christ has nothing more to fear from exterior encounters or from interior difficulties, for these things, far from being an obstacle, serve only ''to root it more deeply in the love'' of its Master.*[23]

In this new condition, prepared and confirmed by Christ's grace, Elizabeth rises above the apparent dichotomy between Martha and Mary. Contemplation and action are peacefully coexistent in her life, not as two separate moments, but as one unique act of love in, through and with Christ the Savior. In this regard she writes:

*I thought of you when, in Father Vallée, I read these words
on contemplation: "the contemplative is a being who lives in
the radiance of the face of Christ; who enters into the
mystery of God, not in the light that shines from human
thought but in that shed by the word of the Word Incarnate."*

*Do you not have the same passionate longing to listen to
him? At times one feels so strongly the need of silence that
one would wish to do nothing but remain like Mary at the
Master's feet, eager to hear all, to penetrate ever more
deeply into that mystery of charity which he came to reveal to
us. Yet do you not find that in action, when we are ap-
parently doing Martha's work, the soul can remain buried in
its contemplation like Mary, staying very near to him? It is
thus that I understand the apostolate both for the Carmelite
and for the priest. In this way, both can radiate God and give
him to souls if they remain at the source of divine life. It
seems to me that we must draw very close to the Master,
commune with his soul, become identified with its every
movement, and then go forth as he did to do the will of his
Father.*[24]

In Elizabeth's life as a contemplative nun, there was perfect
harmony between contemplation and action rather than an artificial
division because both were united under the bonds of charity.
Permeated with the love that is God, pervaded by his grace, and
animated by the Holy Spirit, she felt the need to give all this to
others in prayer since she had a sense of union with them in their
problems, toil, joys and anxieties. Both an apostle and a Carmelite,
she realized that the only person who can have an apostolic impact
on the world is one who is steadfastly united with God, as was the
Blessed Virgin.

I want to work for the glory of God, and for that I must be wholly filled with him. Then I shall be all-powerful. A look, a desire will become a prayer that cannot be resisted and that can obtain everything, since it is, so to speak, God whom we offer to God. May our souls be but one in him. While you carry him to souls, I, like Mary Magdalene, will stay close to the Master in silent adoration, asking him to render your work fruitful in souls. Apostle, Carmelite; it is all one.[25]

In Elizabeth's contemplative life there is a fruitful blending of the vertical and horizontal dimensions of love. Consequently, her practice of prayer is not totally unworldly or directed against the world; rather, it is authentically Christian; that is, it is engrafted on Christ, as was that of the Virgin Mary. Moreover, Mary possessed a perfect symbiosis of action and contemplation that was based on a humility and simplicity that attracted the divine glance to herself.

In what peace, in what recollection Mary lent herself to everything she did! How even the most trivial things were divinized by her! For through it all the Virgin remained the adorer of the gift of God! This did not prevent her from spending herself outwardly when it was a matter of charity; the Gospel tells us that Mary went in haste to the mountains of Judea to visit her cousin Elizabeth. Never did the ineffable vision that she contemplated within herself in any way diminish her outward charity.[26]

As an heir to the Carmelite tradition and following the example of the Blessed Virgin and the Carmelite saints, Elizabeth accentuated the apostolic aspect of charity, understood as comprising mystical union with God and disinterested service for neighbor. She repeats several times in her writings that she had found the *unum necessarium*, which is God, and she was immersed entirely in his divine light and love. Having been made a sharer in the hidden secrets of

God, her life was not only "an advent that prepares for the incarnation in souls,"[27]   but also a prolongation of the salvific mission of Christ and the Blessed Virgin in the ordinary duties of her daily life.

On the anniversary of the religious profession of one of the nuns, Elizabeth presented her with a scapular, accompanied by a "message from the Blessed Virgin," addressed to the nun and to all Carmelites:

> *On entering into the world, Jesus made the first oblation of himself to the Father in my arms; and now he asks me to receive your oblation. I bring you a scapular as a pledge of my benevolence and my love and, at the same time as a sign of the mystery that will be accomplished in you. My daughter, I come to complete your being* clothed in Christ Jesus *so that you may* walk in him, *the royal way, the luminous path; that you may be* rooted in him *in the depths of the abyss, with the Father and the Spirit of love; that you may be* built upon him, *your Rock.*[28]

In response to Mary's pledge of love, Elizabeth records in her *Diary* on January 27, 1900, that she had consecrated herself anew to the Mother of Carmel and had entrusted to her her innocence and virtue. At the same time she resolved to pass her life on earth in imitation of the Blessed Virgin — in silence and discretion but no less efficaciously and fruitfully in service to her neighbor.[29]

──────────── FOOTNOTES ────────────

1 Elizabeth of the Trinity, *Complete Works*, Vol. I, tr. A. Kane, O.C.D., ICS Publications, Washington, D.C., 1984, pp. 110-111. The quotation is from the writings of Ruysbroeck.
2 Letter to Canon Angles, July, 1906. Elizabeth received the Carmelite habit on the feast of the Immaculate Conception, 1901.
3 St. Peter Chrysologus, Sermon 98, tr. G. Ganss in *The Fathers of the Church*, Vol. 17, Catholic University Press, Washington, D.C., 1953. Cf. Mt 13:31-32.
4 *Complete Works*, p. 160.
5 *Ibid.*
6 *Ibid.*
7 Letter to G. de Gemeaux, August, 1902.
8 Letter to her sister, November, 1903.
9 Letter to Mlle. d'Anthès, 1906.
10 Letter to Abbé Chevignard, June, 1905.
11 *Complete Works*, p. 110.
12 *Ibid.*, p. 141. Cf. Jn 1:18.
13 Letter to Abbé Chevignard, June, 1903.
14 Letter to her mother, August, 1904.
15 *Complete Works*, p. 141.
16 *Ibid.*, pp. 160-161. *Janua Coeli* (Gate of Heaven) is from the Litany of the Blessed Virgin and the title that Elizabeth applied to Mary most frequently. Scripture quotes are from Jn 19:27, Col 1:24, and Jn 19:30.
17 Letter to F. de Sourdon, 1905.
18 Letter to Abbé Beaubis, June, 1904.
19 Letter to Abbé Chevignard, December, 1904. Cf. Ep 3:17-19.
20 Letter to G. de Gemeaux, May, 1906.
21 Elizabeth of the Trinity, *Diary*, February 20, 1899.
22 Letter to Mlle. A. de Bobet, September, 1906.
23 *Complete Works*, pp. 156-157.
24 Letter to Abbé Chevignard, December, 1905.
25 Letter to Abbé Beaubis, June, 1904.
26 *Complete Works*, pp. 110-111.
27 Letter to Abbé Chevignard, December, 1905.
28 Note given to a nun on the anniversary of her religious profession.
29 Letter to Abbé Chevignard, November, 1903.

CHAPTER   THREE

CONFORMABLE TO THE IMAGE OF HIS SON

As a pilgrim on earth, Elizabeth, on receiving the gift of God, manifested herself as an authentic contemplative like the Blessed Virgin Mary. She was intimately united — or, better yet, interiorly assimilated — to Christ, the Word incarnate, and through him she was able to penetrate into the intimate life of the Trinity. The life of the Trinity that was hers through the grace of baptism developed in her through the grace of Christ and the power of the Holy Spirit. Through the union of her soul with Christ she was able to "enter into the movement of his divine spirit and to have as an ideal that of doing the will of the Father, who has loved us with an eternal love."[1]   The interior life of the young Carmelite was a continual expression of the divine action within her. The more receptive she was, the more she grew in faith, hope and charity, drawn as she was by the power of the Holy Spirit who gradually and progressively formed her according to the image of the Son.

The spiritual incarnation of the Word in Elizabeth marks the beginning of a long and delightful exchange of love between herself and the triune God. She described it as "that *admirabile commercium*, of which we sing in the beautiful liturgy; an intimacy like that between spouse and bride."[2]   By means of this close relationship the young Carmelite, predestined to be made conformable to Christ, becomes a daughter in the Son and hence a perfect image of the Word, a praise of glory in the bosom of the Trinity, and the faithful bride of the divine Spouse. Elevated by the grace of Christ and inserted into the community of the Trinity, she is moved by the Holy Spirit, who evokes in her the love of the Father and enables her to experience herself as a daughter and coheir with Christ, with whom she desires to die in order to be definitively glorified.

So far as Elizabeth's spiritual life converged on the mystery of Christ it was nourished by the theology of St. Paul and the Carmelite tradition as expounded by St. Teresa of Avila and St. John of the Cross. Indeed, before being Trinitarian, her mysticism is Christocentric and through Christ she is led to the transforming union with the three divine Persons. Thanks to Elizabeth, we have once more in the Church the manifestation of a particular way of tending to perfection. Consequently, her life is yet another invitation to respond to the universal call to the perfection of charity and to see this vocation of all Christians in a wider context.

The Word Incarnate, The Way To The Trinity

THE MYSTICAL EXPERIENCE of the Carmelite of Dijon is primarily concerned with transcending earthly reality, not precisely as an escape, but to be able to enter into total union with God through the mediation of Christ. Like St. Teresa of Avila, her mother and teacher, Elizabeth understood that it is only through the sacred humanity of Christ, the sacrament of every mystical experience, that the souls in glory can enjoy the "repose of the abyss because they contemplate God in the simplicity of his essence."[3]

Christ the God-man is not therefore an abstract reality but a vital and active protagonist in Elizabeth's spiritual growth and development. It is precisely in and through the incarnate Word that the life of the Trinity given her at baptism can develop.

It seems to me that we must draw very close to the Master,
commune with his soul, become identified with its every

movement, and then go forth as he did to do the will of his Father. I would like to be "buried with Christ in God," to lose myself in that Trinity which will one day be our vision and, in its brilliance immerse myself in the abyss of the mystery.[4]

To walk in Christ Jesus, after becoming totally detached from self; to follow faithfully in his footsteps; to imitate his actions — all this was for Elizabeth a way of immersing herself ever more deeply in the mystery of the Trinity. This is the vocation to which she was called by Christ himself: "My Master . . . wants to dwell in me with the Father and his Spirit of love, so that, in the words of the beloved disciple, I may have 'communion' with them."[5]

To that end, Christ recommended that she withdraw into the interior of her soul in an atmosphere of divine and virginal silence in order to savor his salvific and vivifying presence. This was the point of convergence for her loving dedication, her blind faith and her adoring contemplation.

"Remain in me." It is the Word of God who gives this order, expresses his wish. Remain in me, not for a few moments, a few hours which must pass away, but "remain" permanently, habitually. Remain in me, pray in me, adore in me, love in me, suffer in me, work and act in me. Remain in me so that you may be able to encounter anyone or anything; penetrate further still into these depths. This is truly the "solitude into which God wants to allure the soul so that he may speak to it," as the prophet sang.[6]

Her experience of divine union with, in and through Christ enabled Elizabeth to rise to the sphere of the supernatural and to perform actions that are no longer simply human but in accordance with the Spirit of Christ. And in the radically transforming union with the three Persons, achieved through her relationship to Christ, the sanctification of Elizabeth is achieved. It is a continuous process that plunges her ever more deeply into the mystery of the triune God.

He is in us in order to sanctify us. So let us ask him to be himself our sanctity. When our Lord was on earth, we are told in the Gospel, "virtue went out from him." At his touch, the sick recovered their health, the dead were restored to life. Now he is ever living — in his adorable Sacrament. And in our souls. He it is who has said: "If any man love me, he will keep my word, and my Father will love him; and we will come to him and make our abode with him." [7]

Apart from Christ there is neither sanctity nor salvation — terms which for Elizabeth are synonymous — because God, in his eternal designs, has willed to "restore all things in Christ." [8] Consequently, all who desire to attain perfection must live in Jesus Christ, be rooted in him, be built up in him, strengthened in faith through him, constantly growing in him through thanksgiving. [9]

Through the sacred humanity of Christ, Elizabeth attained to the very essence of God. In a mystical way she experienced the inner life of the Trinity and the mutual relations among the Father, the Son and the Holy Spirit. She contemplated the three Persons of the Trinity and adored the ineffable divine love that circulated among them. [10] Drawn as if by force into that circle of the divine love of the Persons of the Trinity, Elizabeth gradually underwent a mystical transformation, taking on the mode of the life and love of the Trinity. She then addressed an ardent plea to the Holy Spirit: "O consuming Fire, Spirit of love, 'come upon me,' and create in my soul a kind of incarnation of the Word; that I may be another humanity for him in which he can renew his whole Mystery." [11]

It is the mystery of Christ, hypostatically united to the Word, that gathers the members of the mystical body in a continuous contemplative gaze of the heavenly Father. Through Christ and under the guidance of the Holy Spirit, Elizabeth, while conscious of ecclesial solidarity, knew how to strive only for the realization of her ideal of love, namely, to be firmly established in the bosom of the Trinity.

> *Oh! How beautiful is this creature thus stripped, freed from self!. . . . It ascends, it rises above the senses, above nature; it transcends itself; it goes beyond every joy and every pain and passes through the clouds, not stopping until it has penetrated* " into the interior" *of him whom it loves and who himself will give it "the repose of the abyss." And all that without leaving the holy fortress!. . . It is also without leaving it that the soul will live, like the immutable Trinity, in an* eternal present, *"adoring him always because of himself," and becoming by an always more simple, more unitive gaze, "the splendor of his glory," that is, the unceasing praise of glory of his adorable perfections.* [12]

Thus does the Carmelite mystic become a sharer in the selfsame love that circulates within the community of the three divine Persons, to live this love not only in her own interior but among her fellow religious.

A Life Like That Of Christ

IN ORDER to realize her vocation as praise of glory in the bosom of the Trinity, Elizabeth found no better way than to conform to the image of Christ the God-man. Since St. Paul teaches that those whom God has foreknown, he has predestined to be conformed to the image of his Son, Elizabeth concludes: "It is important then that I study this divine Model so as to identify myself so closely with him that I may unceasingly reveal him to the eyes of the Father." [13]   The ultimate goal for which she strives with all her might is to be made conformable to the perfect image of the Father, namely, the Word in his redemptive incarnation. It is by sharing in the mystery of Christ's docile obedience to the will of his Father that Elizabeth becomes a ''new creature'' (Col 3:10) and regains the right to God's glory (Rm 3:23): the manifestation of his liberating power, his salvific presence, and his love that generates a new life. Then, at the end of time, ''the Holy One of God will have been glorified in this soul, for he will have destroyed everything there to 'clothe it with himself,' and it will have loved in reality the words of the Precursor: 'He must increase and I must decrease.' ''[14]   In other words, the young Carmelite was convinced that in the measure that she died to self, the image of the resurrected Christ would be more clearly manifested in her.

In the process of her assimilation to Christ she became a sharer in the most intimate sentiments of Jesus in relation to his Father. ''I feel that all the treasures hidden in the soul of Christ are mine and I feel rich indeed.''[15]   In her efforts to penetrate the movements of the soul of Christ, Elizabeth discovers two important aspects of the salvific plan of God: the redemption of mankind and the glory of the Father, both realized in the mystery of the incarnation. Hence, in a letter to the Dominican, Father Vallée, prior to her religious profession, she stated that she felt permeated with the redemptive love of the divine Savior, the guest of her soul. And once she had reached full spiritual maturity, she desired nothing other than the glory of God:

In this marvelous discourse after the Last Supper, which is like the last song of love coming from the soul of the divine Master, Jesus addresses these beautiful words to the Father: ''I have glorified you on earth, I have finished the work of love that you entrusted to me.'' It seems to me that we who belong to him under the title of his spouses and who should be totally identified with him, ought to repeat those words at the end of each day.[16]

In the short span of her life the fervent Carmelite, faithful to her charism and her vocation, is a praise of glory to the Father, the Son and the Holy Spirit, a praise of glory that continues to sing the praises of the Trinity now in eternity.

> *"I live, now not I, but Christ liveth in me!" (Gal 2:20). That is the dream of my Carmelite soul. . . Above all, it is our Lord's dream and I beg him to realize it completely in our souls. Let us strive to be to him another humanity, as it were, in which he may renew his entire mystery. I have asked him to take up his abode in me as Adorer, as Restorer and as Savior. I cannot tell you what peace this gives to my soul, to think that he supplies for my insufficiency and that even though I should fall at every moment, he is there to lift me up and carry me further into himself — into that divine Essence in which we already dwell by grace and in which I long to bury myself so deeply that nothing can ever draw me forth.*[17]

Elizabeth has become a new incarnation of Christ in her life of prayer, immolation and praise of God. Her total assimilation to Christ is the fruit of love, as she herself testifies:

> *"I have come to cast fire upon the earth and how I long to see it burn" (Lk 12:49). It is the Master himself who expresses his desire to see the fire of love enkindled. . . Nothing pleases him so much as to see it "grow." "Now nothing can exalt it so much as to become in some way the equal of God; that is why he demands from the soul the tribute of its love, since the property of love is to make the lover equal to the beloved as much as possible. The soul in possession of this love". . .*
> *"appears on an equal footing with Christ because their mutual affection renders everything common to both." "I have called you my friends because all things that I have heard from my Father I have made known to you" (Jn 15:15).*

But to attain to this love the soul must first be "entirely
surrendered," its "will must be calmly lost in God's will"
so that its "inclinations, its faculties move only in this love
and for the sake of this love.". . . Then "love fills it so
completely, absorbs and protects it . . . that everywhere it
finds the secret of growing in love . . . even in its relations
with the world; in the midst of life's cares it can rightly say:
'My only occupation is loving!' "[18]

In other words, it is necessary that the soul die to self in order to be
born again to a new life with and in the glorified Christ.

"I die daily" (1 Cor 15:31). I decrease, I renounce self
more each day so that Christ may increase in me and be
exalted. . . I live no longer I, but he lives in me. I no longer
want "to live my own life, but to be transformed in Jesus
Christ so that my life may be more divine than human," so
that the Father in bending attentively over me can recognize
the image of his beloved Son in whom he has placed all his
delight.[19]

Through death and love Elizabeth attains to a marvelous mystical
union with Christ wherein she relives his mystery and perpetuates
on earth and in heaven his life of continual praise and eternal glory
of the Trinity. But for the young Carmelite it is not possible to
become fully another Christ without sharing in the mystery of his
cross. Moreover, she knows from personal experience that the
Carmelite vocation is fully realized through conformity to Christ
crucified.

A Carmelite is one who has beheld the Crucified, *who has*
seen him offering himself to his Father as a victim for souls
and, meditating in the light of this great vision of Christ's

charity, has understood the passion of love that filled his soul and has willed to give herself as he did.[20]

To be like the Christ of the cross is for Elizabeth an exigency of supreme love, a love that is verified in every faithful spouse worthy of the name.

"Configuratus morti ejus" ["to be formed after the pattern of his death"] *(Ph 3:10). That is what still haunts me and gives strength to my soul in its suffering. If you knew the sensation of destruction I feel in my whole being! The road to Calvary is opening before me, and I am utterly joyful to walk it as a bride beside my crucified Lord. . . Oh, may I be totally consecrated so that I shall no longer be myself,* but him, *so that in gazing upon me the Father can see that I have been made* conformable to his death, that I suffer that which was wanting in his passion for his body the Church, *and then that I may be immersed in the blood of Christ so that I may be strong with his own strength.*[21]

The union between Elizabeth the bride and the heavenly Bridegroom is completed in the paschal Christ who enables her to live again in her flesh the mystery of his passion, death and resurrection. Conversely, the mystery that she experienced in her flesh facilitated the consummation of her spousal union with Christ and the fulfillment of God's redemptive plan for mankind. This involves the dynamism of the mystical body, projected towards the full realization of the work of redemption. As a responsible member of that immense body, Elizabeth, wracked with suffering, exclaims: "The soul that wants to serve God . . . must be resolved to share *fully* in its Master's passion. It is one of the redeemed who in its turn must redeem other souls, and for that reason it will sing on its lyre: 'I glory in the cross of Jesus Christ' (Gal 6:14). 'With Christ I am nailed to the cross' (Gal 2:19). And again: 'I suffer in my body what is lacking in the passion of Christ for the sake of his body, which is the Church' (Col 1:24).''[22]

And that is what happened. Before closing her eyes on this world, Elizabeth was wracked with the most acute suffering, and yet she experienced the joy and peace of knowing the efficacy of her suffering within the ambit of the communion of saints. She had been tested to the innermost core of her being and clothed in white garments, washed in the blood of the immaculate Lamb of God. Now, after heroic suffering, she contemplates the glory of the Lord face to face. Before being transformed from splendor to splendor in the likeness of the divine Being, she was made conformable to the incarnate Word who died on the cross out of love and rose again.[23]

Christocentric Mysticism

ELIZABETH voluntarily accepted and cooperated with the charism that was freely bestowed on her. Firmly united to the paschal Christ, she discovered inexhaustible resources of grace in order to arrive at a knowledge of the Father and the Son in the Holy Spirit and to be formed into the perfect creature in the measure that she attained to the fullness of Christ (Ep 4:13). The centrality of Christ in her spirituality makes clear, first on the psychological and affective level and then on the theological level the presence of the Word in her soul. On these two supporting columns rests the mystical union of the entire Trinity with the young religious. It is a kind of spiritual symbiosis that transforms and unites the soul to God.

Elizabeth's conformation with Christ previously described is much more than a literal imitation of the incarnate Word, crucified and risen again; it is a sharing in the charity of the Son who is the revelation of the ineffable mystery of the three divine Persons. Therefore, before speaking of the mystical indwelling of the Trinity in Elizabeth, it is fitting to speak of her *Christological mysticism*. The reason is that the divine Being takes possession of the finite heart of his creature through the incarnation, passion and death of Christ and ultimately through the Eucharist of his divine love. The formula, "in Christ Jesus," which often appears in the writings of Elizabeth, is a synthesis of her entire spiritual doctrine and can be understood as the existential response of the young Carmelite to the salvific vocation received from God. Hence her life, lived in absolute and perpetual openness and availability to God, becomes a mystical existence in Jesus Christ, who leads her by the hand beyond the finite and into the realms of the eternal and infinite God.

It seems that Elizabeth first began to experience the divine in the Eucharist, where there is effected an intimate exchange between infinite and finite loves. She states: "It seems to me that nothing so speaks to us of the love in God's heart as the Eucharist. It is union, consummation, God in us and we in him. Is it not heaven on earth?"[24]   And in her *Diary* she wrote as early as 1899: "The Eucharist is the culmination of divine love. Here Jesus gives not only his merits and his sufferings, but all of himself."

Communion with Christ, the Bread of Life, was not limited to the moment of the Eucharistic celebration; it embraced Elizabeth's entire existence. Hers was a vital, fervent and palpitating encounter with the generous love of God. Thus she prays: "Grant that I may live in more complete union with you; that I live only within, in the cell that you have constructed in my heart. In that little part of me where I see and hear you."[25]   In brief, the life of Elizabeth even at that early stage was an unceasing prayer of praise to the Lord from whom nothing could ever separate her: "Lord, let my life be a continual prayer. Grant that nothing may ever distract me from you: neither anxieties nor pleasures nor sufferings. Grant that I may be submerged in you; that I do everything under your gaze."[26]

Elizabeth understood her religious life as a life of permanent union with the Lord. "The life of Carmel," she stated, "is a communion with God from morning till night, from night till morning. If he did not fill our cells, our cloisters, how empty they

would be."[27]   However, this identification with Christ is not an
end in itself; rather, it leads to an experience of union with the
entire Trinity. And to live the very life of the Trinity, that Jesus
came to bring to us, was something indescribable for Elizabeth;
and yet Christ had said that he came to bring us life and to bring it
more abundantly.[28]   This is possible because Christ is God and
because in suffering with him she can know him as God and man
and be made conformable to him. But it is precisely through his
divinity that she finds the means of reaching her "Three" in their
mystery of love.

> *"By baptism," says St. Paul, "we have been united to Jesus*
> *Christ." And again: "God seated us together in heaven in*
> *Christ Jesus, that he might show in the ages to come the*
> *riches of his grace." And further on: "You are no longer*
> *guests or strangers, but you belong to the city of saints and*
> *the house of God." The Trinity — this is our dwelling, our*
> *"home," the Father's house that we must never leave. The*
> *Master said one day: "The slave does not remain with the*
> *household forever, but the son remains there forever" (St.*
> *John).*[29]

The presence of Christ — and more precisely that of God one and
three — in the soul of Elizabeth resulted in an ineffable mystical
experience that we could call *Christo-Trinitarian*. She disposed
herself for it by an ascetical effort to conform herself to the
incarnate Word, who died and rose again for our salvation. Hers is
undoubtedly a spousal mysticism because influenced by the
mystics of the Rhineland and the Low Countries, but especially
because it is based on the new covenant in Christ, expressed in
nuptial symbols. In other words, in the economy of salvation, at the
center of which is the incarnation, death and glorification of the
Word, the triune God invites Elizabeth to make a total gift of self in
order to create in her not only the image of the Son but to lead her to

a union that is a divinization of her earthly existence. The communion of life between God the spouse and Elizabeth the bride demands constant availability and total dedication, to which the young religious responds generously by one act of love that encompassed her entire life. The initiative, of course, came from the loving Trinity, which also provided the ideal conditions for her acceptance and response.

Everything in Elizabeth's life speaks to her of the perfection of the Trinity, in addition to the Son, the Word of God. The sign of the cross, for example, is a vocalized remembrance of the action of the Trinity in the soul of the human person, just as all creation is a vestige or reflection of the presence of the Trinity throughout the universe. Everything speaks of the triune God to the soul that is in harmony with the transcendent Being. And if it is true, as it is, that the soul must listen in silence to God, who speaks and makes himself present in us and around us in a thousand ways, it is also true that the adoring response of Elizabeth in her mystical experience is a mixture of joy and sacrifice precisely because her soul is not yet completely free to enjoy the infinite Trinity face to face.

It is the law here below that sacrifice accompanies joy. The good God wants to remind us that we have not yet arrived at the terminus of happiness, but we are directed towards it and he himself wants to lead us to it in his arms. Up above, dear sister, he will fill all our emptiness. In the meanwhile, let us live in the heaven of our soul.[30]

When the Trinity takes possession of a soul through the mediation of the Word incarnate, as in the case of Elizabeth, it causes indescribable joy but at the same time suffering. The reason is that the infinite Trinity is restricted, or one might say obstructed, by the finiteness of the human person. And since the individual cannot encompass in a mystical embrace the infinite Being that is drawing it to union with the Trinity, the soul suffers and groans but waits and hopes, striving to pass beyond self to the full transforming union with the triune God.

It is the contemplative experience in the culminating phase of Elizabeth's practice of prayer that provides her with an intuition full of love. It is a new way of experiencing the triune God. In this phase of her spiritual life God gives himself totally as a community of love to the young Carmelite to the degree that she gives herself generously to the action of the transforming Spirit. There is, so to speak, an *interpenetration* of the very personhood of her beloved divine Persons. Such an experience does not increase her speculative knowledge of God, but it helps her to understand the limits of her own human nature, Not only that, but since an authentic religious experience should find an outlet in one's relations with others, the contemplative experience of Elizabeth is shown to be genuine because her life was rich in operative charity.

In other words, we can say that the mystery that Elizabeth lived in her interior life is the mystery of the covenant in its nuptial expression: *God with you, in Christ Jesus*. She has become another Christ because all that she is, all that she has, and all that she will be is a gift from God. Redeemed and saved by Christ, she gives herself to him, she surrenders herself to him, she welcome him with the freedom of her virginal consecration. Such is her nuptial relationship with Christ in the Spirit, and because of that she is also spouse of the triune God, constituted as such by the Spirit of Christ.

FOOTNOTES

1 Letter to Mme. Angles, September, 1902.
2 Letter to Mme. Angles, November, 1905.
3 Elizabeth of the Trinity, *Complete Works*, Vol. I, tr. A. Kane, O.C.D. ICS Publications, Washington, D.C., 1984, p. 143.
4 Letter to Abbé Chevignard, February, 1903.
5 *Complete Works*, pp. 161-162.
6 *Ibid.*, pp. 94-95. Cf. Ho 2:16.
7 Letter to Mme. Angles, November, 1904. Scripture quotations are from Mk 5:30 and Jn 14:23.
8 Ep 1:10.
9 *Complete Works*, p. 156.
10 *Ibid.*, p. 98.
11 From Elizabeth's famous prayer to the Trinity, composed on November 21, 1904. Cf. *Ibid.*, p. 183.
12 *Complete Works*, p.162.
13 *Ibid.*, p. 158.
14 *Ibid.*, pp.159-160.
15 Letter to Abbé Angles, September, 1901.
16 Letter to Mme. Angles, January, 1906. Cf. Jn 17:4.
17 Letter to Abbé Chevignard, November, 1904.
18 *Complete Works*, p. 99. Quotations are from St. John of the Cross, *Spiritual Canticle*, Stanza 28.
19 *Complete Works*, pp. 97-98. Quotations are from St. John of the Cross, *Spiritual Canticle*, Stanza 12.
20 Letter to Mme. de Gemeaux, August, 1902.
21 Letter to Abbé Angles, July, 1906.
22 *Complete Works*, p. 146.
23 *Ibid.*, pp. 146-147.
24 Letter to Abbé Chevignard, June, 1903.
25 *Diary*, May 24, 1900.
26 *Diary*, January 27, 1900.
27 Letter to Mlle. F. de Sourdon, 1904.
28 Letter to Abbé Chevignard, April, 1904.
29 *Complete Works*, p. 94. Scripture quotations are from Gal 3:27, Ep 2:6-7,Ep 2:19, Jn 8:35.
30 Letter to her sister, August, 1904.

CHAPTER FOUR

TO DIE IN ORDER TO LIVE

ANYONE who would experience Christ and God one and three
cannot be exempted from embracing the cross, for this is a require-
ment of that love which unites two into one. To live entirely for
God, one must experience the nothingness, the *nada*, of self and of
all things else. Thirsting as she did for the absolute which is God,
Elizabeth, in conformity with biblical and Carmelite tradition, had
to pass through an interior and exterior desert in order to achieve
union with God: solitude and silence, separation from the world,
mortification — in a word, *kenosis*. This passage, traversed in faith
and with courage, created in her soul the dispositions necessary for
the intervention of the sanctifying Spirit. Then the passive purgation — an important phase of her spiritual life — refined, purified
and simplified her soul in the crucible of the fire of love that
proceeds from the Holy Spirit.

Under the tutelage of the third Person of the Trinity Elizabeth
saw clearly her specific vocation: to live in close intimacy with God
in her own interior, in the deepest center of her being, after having
been emptied of self. It is there that the young Carmelite, totally
transfigured, finally establishes herself, not to withdraw into a
pleasant retreat within herself, but in pure contemplation to adore
her Creator within herself and in all creation. Intimately penetrated
by the Trinity in a union of love, Elizabeth blended the ascetical
and mystical phases of her spiritual life in perfect harmony,

without favoring or giving precedence to one or the other. In view of her strong desire for full identification with Christ, the Holy Spirit takes up and completes the work of purgation in the dark night of the senses and spirit so that she can, as a new creation, enjoy the eternal happiness of the ineffable and undivided Trinity.

The action of the Holy Spirit not only purges her of every stain and imperfection of heart and mind, but he simplifies her interiorly, that is, he brings her to that interior disposition called ''simplicity of soul,'' which is the one best disposition for penetrating the hidden secrets of the simple Being that is God. Moreover, such spiritual simplicity really constitutes a new way of living, which Elizabeth accepted and carried out in the ordinary task of daily life. The life of Elizabeth thus becomes a witness to the new being with which she has been gifted through the power of the Holy Spirit. Death for her is not the end of life but a passage to life.

The Desert In Carmel

THE CONSTITUTIVE ELEMENTS of the striving for sanctity are self-renunciation and union with God. In the life of the Carmelite of Dijon these two aspects constitute the one act of dedication to the absolute which is God. Carmel may therefore be considered a desert not only because it provides the means for a total detachment from self but also because it disposes one for an experience of the divine life.

Speaking through his prophet, the Lord said: ''I will lead her into solitude and speak to her heart'' (Ho 2:14). The soul has entered into this vast solitude in which God will make himself heard. ''His word,'' St. Paul says, ''is living and active, and more penetrating than a two-edged sword: extending even to the division of soul and spirit, even of joints and marrow'' (Heb 4:12). It is his word then that will directly achieve the work of stripping in the soul; for it has

*this particular characteristic, that it effects and creates what
it intends, providing however that the soul consents to let this
be done.*[1]

To pass through the desert means for Elizabeth to regain the faith of
a former time and to experience once again the encounter with
God. Accordingly, there coexist in the desert experience a chaotic
element and a sacred element, in the sense that to advance through
the desert means to live again symbolically in one's own flesh the
moment of creation and at the same time to let oneself be moulded
by God and transformed by him into a new creature.

Since the desert is a place of silence and solitude, one must be
quiet and place oneself in a posture of listening to God, who
communicates himself to the soul. As an intrepid Carmelite,
Elizabeth is convinced that God does not communicate himself to
her in words or in beautiful human language, but in the silence of
her interior life. Here she follows and quotes the advice of St. John
of the Cross, who states that the soul must observe silence and
absolute solitude so that the omnipotent God can realize all his
desires in it.[2]   But to achieve this, God must prepare in the soul "a
serene dwelling-place, echoing the great silence that exists in
God."[3]   In a word, "a Carmelite's life is silence."[4]

Once having entered Carmel, Elizabeth was strongly attracted
to the solitude of the life and she would have liked to pass her entire
religious life "alone with the Alone," a phrase that recurs frequently in her writings. Such an attitude was fully in conformity
with the Primitive Rule composed by St. Teresa of Avila, which
stated:

*All the time that they are not with the community or occupied
in its duties, let each sister stay in her own cell or hermitage
assigned to her by the Prioress. In short, they must stay in
the place of their retirement, doing some work — except on*

feastdays; thus in solitude fulfilling the injunction of the Rule, that each one shall remain alone.[5]

In such a desert solitude Elizabeth was able to imitate more perfectly and love and contemplate more intensely the hidden life of Jesus, a life of hidden union between the Father and the Son. Moreover, in company with the silent Christ she could penetrate the divine silence of the Father and the Holy Spirit. She expresses these sentiments in one of her letters:

On the mountain of Carmel, in silence, in solitude, in a prayer that never ceases because it continues through all else, the Carmelite lives as though already in heaven, by God alone. The selfsame God who will one day be the cause of her beatitude and will fully satisfy her in glory, is already giving himself to her. He never leaves her: he dwells within her soul; more than that, the two become but one. *And so* she hungers for silence *in order to be always listening, to penetrate ever more deeply into his infinite Being. She is identified with him whom she loves.*[6]

Her stance was that of a silent contemplative: "At times one feels so strongly the need of silence that one would wish to do nothing but remain like Magdalene at the Master's feet, eager to hear all, to penetrate ever more deeply into that mystery of charity that he came to reveal to us."[7]   She thus reaches God through the God-man and shares in his mystery of love, which is revealed in silence. To immerse herself in silence is for her a means of self-annihilation at every moment so that she can let herself be pervaded by the divine Word. In such a state of silent recollection she does not inquire about her own spiritual progress; she simply lets herself be fashioned in her own interior and to be led to a new mode of existence by the Holy Spirit. Her silence generates in her a knowledge of the love of God and a simplicity and purity of heart that open to her the doors of contemplation.

> *My Rule tells me: "In silence will your strength be." It seems to me, therefore, that to keep one's strength for the Lord is to unify one's whole being by means of interior silence, to collect all one's powers in order to "employ" them in "the one work of love," to have this "single eye" which allows the light of God to enlighten us.*[8]

Having been gifted with simplicity of spirit in order to know the unique simple Being who is God, Elizabeth reduced her religious life to a continuous dialogue with the Alone after she had definitely renounced her own ego. Then, free at last from every human attachment, she lived in the triune God because, buried with Christ, she had silenced the pressing demands of the flesh. Such was the ultimate meaning of silence for Elizabeth, so similar to the *nada* of St. John of the Cross, a silence that created in her heart a vast contemplative quiet.

> *The divine Being lives in an eternal, immense solitude. He never leaves it, though concerning himself with the needs of his creatures, for he never leaves himself; and this solitude is nothing else than his divinity.*

> *So that nothing may draw me out of this beautiful silence within, I must always maintain the same dispositions, the same solitude, the same withdrawal, the same stripping of self! If my desires, my fear, my joys or my sorrows, if all the movements proceeding from these "four passions" are not perfectly directed to God, I will not be solitary; there will be noise within me. There must be peace, "sleep of the powers," the unity of being.*[9]

In this state of spiritual poverty or, if one wishes, of forgetfulness
and total spoliation of self, which is not "an external separation
from external things, but a solitude of spirit, a detachment from all
that is not God,"[10]   Elizabeth delights in the divine perfections in
peace and unity of spirit. Carried beyond all things to communion
with the Trinity, she is transformed into the divine image; and this,
says Elizabeth, is the contemplative life, a contemplation that leads
to possession. She then quotes from Ruysbroeck: "Now this simple possession is eternal life savored in the unfathomable abode. It
is there, beyond reason, that the profound tranquillity of the divine
immutability awaits us."[11]

Enveloped in the holy silence of the Trinity, Elizabeth lets God
impress himself on her soul and transform her into himself. There
is nothing in the world that can separate her from this intimate
mystical union that was established in silence between God and
herself. Nothing else is of any real interest to her. She lives in a
state of spiritual indifference in which God alone matters to her —
God and his love. Everything else is secondary and marginal.

*It seems to me the Master had that in mind when he spoke to
Mary Magdalene [sic.] of the "unum necessarium" ["one
thing necessary" (Lk 10:42)]. How well that great saint
understood this! "The eye of her soul enlightened by faith"
recognized her God beneath the veil of his humanity; and in
silence, in the unity of her powers, "she listened to what he
told her." She could sing, "My soul is always in my hands,"
and also this little word: "nescivi"! Yes, she knew nothing
but him! There could be noise and excitement around her:
"Nescivi"! They could accuse her: "Nescivi"! Neither
empty self-esteem nor exterior things could draw her out of
her "sacred silence."*

*It is the same for the soul that has entered into the "fortress
of holy recollection"; the eye of its soul, opened in the light*

> *of faith, discovers its God present, living within it; in turn it*
> *remains so present to him, in beautiful simplicity, that he*
> *guards it with a jealous care. Then disturbances from with-*
> *out and tempests from within may arise; its self-esteem may*
> *be wounded:* "Nescivi"! *God may hide himself, withdraw*
> *his sensible grace:* "Nescivi"! *Or, as St. Paul writes: "For*
> *love of him I have forfeited everything" (Ph 3:8). Then the*
> *Master is free, free to flow into the soul, to give himself*
> *"according to his measure." And the soul thus simplified,*
> *unified, becomes the throne of the unchanging One, since*
> *"unity is the throne of the Holy Trinity."* [12]

Such is the asceticism of silence, which for Elizabeth was not only
a means associated with solitude and recollection, but also constituted an ideal stance of total availability in which the triune God
could take complete possession of her life.

Elizabeth's Ascetical Life

IT IS NOT DIFFICULT to discern in the life and teaching of the young
Carmelite the way of asceticism that the Lord suggested in order to
lead her to intimate union with the divine Persons. Essentially her
method of asceticism consisted in a constant forgetfulness of self in
order to live in humility and in simplicity of heart. Thus, she wrote
in one of her letters: "To forget oneself, to put oneself aside, to
take no account of oneself, to look only at the Master . . . this
transports the soul to serene heights."[13]

Another element of her asceticism is the practice of mortification, daily acts of renunciation of her own ego in order to give
herself completely to God. "Sacrifice . . . and renunciation. This
should be the great law for every Christian life. . . It presupposes
great mortification because in order to be constantly united with
him, one must know how to give all to him."[14] There are in
addition the physical sufferings that she imposed on herself as

expressions of love in order to mortify herself and thus gradually attain a total detachment from self. Before entering Carmel she wrote in her *Diary*: "Since it is practically impossible for me to impose other sufferings on myself, I must somehow convince myself that physical and bodily suffering is only a means . . . for achieving interior mortification and complete self-detachment."[15] In a word, we can say that Elizabeth's ascetical effort tended towards a *kenosis* that involved a total annihilation of self.

> *This is the way set forth; we have only to strip off self to follow it as God wills! To strip off self, to die to self, to lose sight of self. It seems to me the Master meant this when he said: "If anyone wants to follow me, let him take up his cross and deny himself."* [16]

Forgetfulness of self, the practice of mortification, voluntary and deliberate acceptance of suffering, the struggle to correct her character,[17] the immolation of self in silence, her detachment from self and the world before and after entering Carmel — all these things were willed and practiced not for themselves but for love of the Crucified. "To attain to the self-annihilation, the disdain for themselves and the love of suffering that permeated the souls of the saints, it seems necessary to remain a long time in contemplation of God, crucified out of love."[18]   In this sweet but painful union with Christ, Elizabeth found the courage to accept the active purgation, and God gave her the strength to accept the purifying suffering.

The foregoing phase of the ascetical life of Elizabeth was followed by the night of faith, a purification initiated and carried out directly under the Holy Spirit. In this night the soul is not completely inactive but it collaborates in the world of interior transformation by accepting whatever God wills, and doing so in an attitude of intense faith. Cast into total aridity and deprived of her most cherished affections and sensible satisfactions formerly experienced in her prayer and works of virtue, Elizabeth for the first time found herself completely abandoned, in order to give proof of her faith, her love, and her hope. She was being called to live a life that is no longer human but supernatural, and this is the secret of her progress in the spiritual life. "To arrive at the ideal life of the soul I believe that it is necessary to live in the supernatural, that is, no longer to act on the natural level. It is necessary to realize that God is found here, within the deepest part of us, and to face everything with him." [19]

The process of purification is typical of all progress in the spiritual life and it began for Elizabeth during her novitiate when, after a period of consolations, she had to have recourse to the support of her faith in order to follow God's will in her daily life and not fall into the routine of mediocrity. During this period she wrote: "It is no longer only a veil that hides me, but a thick wall. It is difficult, after having experienced him so close. But I am ready to remain in this state for as long as it pleases my Beloved to leave me here, because my faith tells me that he is near me now and always. Besides, what good are sweetness and consolation if they are not he?" [20] It was only by faith in the presence of God, who concealed himself to put her to the test, that Elizabeth was able to sustain her intimacy with the three divine Persons in prayer. Conversely, her prayer, practiced in all simplicity and trust, strengthened her faith to such an extent that she conducted herself like an infant that rests in the arms of one that it loves without actually feeling anything. In spite of the rigors of the test to which God submitted her, she remained always certain of his love for her.

In addition to its purifying effects, Elizabeth's purgation also produced the positive effect of strengthening her for the encounter with Christ during the period of prayerful waiting. In this time of vigil, says Elizabeth, "we believe in *love*, with St. John, and from the moment that we possess this within us, what matter the nights that can obscure our heaven, what matter if Jesus seems to sleep? Oh, let us also rest at his side, let us be calm and quiet, let us not

wake him but await him in faith."[21] The ascetical effort of
Elizabeth consisted in waiting in faith for the purifying night to pass
and for the luminous dawning of union with the triune God. What
matters during the time of vigil is to love with a love that burns
away everything that is not God and to hope that he will come to
save her, strong only in the faith that illumines the darkness that
envelops her soul in this purgation.

*Here faith, the beautiful light of faith appears. It alone
should light my way as I go to meet the Bridegroom. . . I must
immerse myself in "the sacred darkness" by putting all my
powers in darkness and emptiness; then I will meet my
Master, and "the light that surrounds him like a cloak" (Ps
103:2) will envelop me also, for he wants his bride to be
luminous with his light.*[22]

Elizabeth spent the last days of her life in this way. Suffering to the
limit of her endurance and even deprived of the Eucharist, she
could rightly say that she found her Bridegroom on the cross. But
the cross is a source of life, not death; in fact, it was only in passing
through suffering and purgation that she could hope to enjoy the
peace of the just in the eternal contemplation of the ineffable
mystery of the Trinity.

Death And Resurrection

TO LIVE LOVE, especially in times of trial, this was Elizabeth's
program and her constant effort. To succeed in this, she accepted
and endured difficult physical and moral trials under the guidance
of the Holy Spirit, who willed to transform her into a new creation.
But such an interior renewal was possible only after a spiritual
death.

It is only by the path of renunciation that one can reach the divine goal. That is how we die to self and give place to him alone in our heart. . . Our Lord said to Nicodemus: "I tell you most solemnly, unless a man is born from above, he cannot see the kingdom of God" (Jn 3:3). Let us therefore be renewed in the interior of our souls, "stripping off our old self and putting on the new self in the image of its creator" (Col 3:10). All this should be done in sweetness and simplicity, separating ourselves from everything that is not God. Then the soul has no more fears or desires; its will is lost entirely in that of God, and since this is what produces union, it can exclaim: "I live now, not I, but Christ lives in me" (Gal 2:20). [23]

Elizabeth knew that after death comes the fullness of life and she saw the paschal Christ in his salvific death on the cross as the prelude to the resurrection. Sharing in this mystery of death — mystically but nonetheless really — the young Carmelite is automatically projected into the dynamism of a new life in which she experiences God in order to glorify him. So efficacious is her insertion into the paschal mystery of Christ through faith that the life of Jesus is reflected in her actions and attitude. Her very existence is, as it were, transfigured, exalted and divinized.

What I desire is to know him, the Christ, and to share in his sufferings and be made conformable to his death. St. Paul refers to the mystical death in which the soul is annihilated and is so forgetful of self that it ultimately dies in God in order to be transformed in him. [24]

As a victim of love, Elizabeth endeavored each day to die to self. With St. Paul, she could exclaim: "I die daily!"

This teaching of death to self, my dear Frances, which is the law for each Christian soul because Christ has said: "If anyone will come after me, let him take up his cross and deny himself," this teaching, which seems so austere, is rather one of delightful sweetness when one looks at the terminus of that death, which is God's life replacing our life of sin and misery. [25]

Thus, in dying to self moment by moment, Elizabeth did nothing more than revive her baptismal pledge. Quoting St. Paul's statement to the Colossians: "You are dead and your life is hidden with Christ in God," she adds: "That is the condition: it is necessary to be dead." [26]   To attain and enjoy the life of the everlasting living God, Elizabeth didn't let any occasion pass for death to self, even if it meant she would achieve this only little by little, drop by drop. She accepted this bloodless martyrdom and in fact she desired it intensely in order to arrive at full conformity to the dead and risen Christ. In the last year of her life she wrote in this vein to her mother:

How happy I should be if my Master also desired that I should shed my blood for him! But what I ask of him especially is that martyrdom of love which consumed my holy Mother Teresa, whom the Church proclaims "Victim of divine love." And since the Truth has said that the greatest proof of love is to give one's life for the one loved, I give him mine, that he may do with it as he pleases; if I am not a martyr by blood, I wish to be one for love. [27]

Unable to give witness to Christ by shedding her blood, as did the early Christian martyrs, Elizabeth, enamored of Christ to the point of folly, begged for the unbloody martyrdom of love, which is no less efficacious than the other martyrdom. This was an exigency of her love for him who gave the supreme testimony of his love for mankind by dying on the cross. Her slow and hidden martyrdom, the fruit of her imitation of Christ and prompted by her love for Christ, consisted in living in the desert solitude of her own interior within the walls of the Carmelite cloister. Strong in faith, she patiently endured every spiritual trial; she definitively overcame the enticements of the flesh; she led a life of penance and mortification of her own ego. Hence, the entire religious life of the young Carmelite can be summed up as a martyrdom of love if it is true — as it is — that hers was a life of self-denial for the attainment of sanctity and for total identification with the paschal Christ. Elizabeth realized that such would be her life — one of suffering and mortification — when she passed the night in prayerful vigil on the eve of her religious profession. ''During the night, preceding the great day while I was in choir awaiting the Bridegroom, *I understood that my heaven was beginning on earth; the heaven of faith, with suffering and immolation for him I love.*''[28]

The ascetical phase of Elizabeth's spiritual life was not totally distinct and separated from the mystical; rather, it was a preparation for the mystical intuition of the hidden mystery of Christ in God. It was a necessary passage, like that of the Jews across the Red Sea, to a more perfect God-centered life. From her conformity to the suffering Christ, she gradually passes through faith, hope and charity to the likeness of the glorified Christ, to be led together with him to the innermost and hidden recesses of divine knowledge. Such is the mystical life of Elizabeth: love lived and experienced in this life in suffering while awaiting the full and direct knowledge of God the Father, God the Son and Word incarnate, and God the Holy Spirit, all united in divine charity. It all takes place by means of a mystical death that is a renewal of the paschal mystery that began to be operative in her at the moment of her baptism.

For these souls, the mystical death of which St. Paul spoke yesterday becomes so simple and sweet! They think much

less of the work of destruction and detachment that remains
for them to do than of plunging into the Furnace of love
burning within them, which is none other than the Holy
Spirit, the same love which in the Trinity is the bond between
the Father and his Word. They "enter into him by living
faith, and there, in simplicity and peace" they are "carried
away by him" beyond all things, beyond sensible pleasures,
"into the sacred darkness" and are "transformed into the
divine image."[29]

Both the ascetical and mystical aspects of the spiritual life of
Elizabeth were gifts from the Holy Spirit who thereby confirmed
the grace of baptism by which she was inserted into the dialectic
dynamism of the life and death of Christ. Introduced to a life lived
according to the Spirit, she is purified sufficiently for intimate
union with God. But her insertion into the life of the Trinity was
granted her not so much because of her ascetical efforts but because
by the power of the Holy Spirit she was immersed in the paschal
mystery of Christ. Then, in union with the risen glorious Christ,
she was prepared to live an authentic mystical contemplation of the
Trinity. The action of the Holy Spirit on the heart of Elizabeth not
only purified her and made her holy and immaculate, but it prepared her for her encounter with her heavenly Spouse. In other
words, it directed her towards the fullness of glory wherein her
entire being would share in the life of the Spirit. As St. Paul says:
"All of us who possess the first-fruits of the Spirit, we too groan
inwardly as we wait for our bodies to be set free. For we must be
content to hope that we shall be saved" (Rm 8:23-24). Thus, after
her thorough purgation and renewal, accompanied by growth in the
theological virtues, the soul of Elizabeth was led by the Holy Spirit
to an intimate experience of the divine Being, one in nature and
three in Persons.

————————————— FOOTNOTES —————————————

1 Elizabeth of the Trinity, *Complete Works*, Vol. I, tr. A. Kane, O.C.D., ICS Publications, Washington, D.C., 1984, p. 154.
2 Letter to Abbé Chevignard, June, 1905.
3 Letter to Abbé Chevignard, June, 1903.
4 Letter to her sister, October, 1901.
5 *Primitive Constitutions O.C.D.*, composed by St. Teresa of Jesus, 1567-1568, Curia Generalizia O.C.D., Rome, 1977.
6 Letter to Mlle. G. de Gemeaux, August, 1902.
7 Letter to Abbé Chevignard, February, 1903.
8 *Complete Works*, p. 144. The quotations refer to the Rule of Carmel and St. John of the Cross, *Spiritual Canticle*, Stanza 28.
9 *Complete Works*, p. 153. The words quoted are from St. John of the Cross, *Spiritual Canticle*, Stanza 40, and St. Teresa of Avila, *Life*, Chapter 16.
10 *Complete Works*, p. 96.
11 *Ibid.*, p. 98.
12 *Ibid.*, pp. 142-143. Phrases quoted are from St. John of the Cross, Ruysbroeck and St. Catherine of Siena.
13 Letter to Mlle. A. de Bobet, September, 1906.
14 Letter to Mlle. G. de Gemeaux, May, 1906.
15 *Diary*, February 24, 1899.
16 *Complete Works*, p. 152. Cf. Mk 8:34.
17 Elizabeth wrote in her *Diary* on January 30, 1899: "Today I had the joy of offering to Jesus many sacrifices in order to conquer my predominant fault. . . When I receive an unwarranted correction, I can feel the blood boil in my veins; my whole being rebels."
18 Letter to Abbé Chevignard, November, 1904.
19 Letter to Mlle. F. de Sourdon, October, 1906.
20 Letter to Mlle. M. Gallot, May, 1901.
21 Letter to her sister, August, 1905.
22 *Complete Works*, p. 145.
23 Letter to Mme. Angles, March, 1905.
24 Letter to her sister, July, 1906.
25 Letter to F. de Sourdon, October, 1906. Cf. Mk 8:34.
26 *Complete Works*, p. 148. Cf. Col 3:3.
27 Letter to her mother, June, 1906.
28 Letter to Abbé Angles, July, 1903.
29 *Complete Works*, p. 98. The quotations are from the works of Ruysbroeck.

CHAPTER FIVE

LED BY THE SPIRIT

THE MYSTICAL EXPERIENCE of Elizabeth, like her conformity to the paschal Christ, can be understood only if it is seen as a work of the Holy Spirit. As a true contemplative she could identify the Presence operating in her soul by recalling the theological teaching of St. Paul. In addition to knowing his specific work as third person of the Trinity, she experienced him as the Spirit of love who guides and perfects the operation of God in the soul of his creatures.

Animated by the Spirit, who breathes in the most hidden depths of her interior, she welcomed more and more the unknown promptings of God and thus gave witness in her life of complete docility to the working of the divine Spirit. Hers was a continuous act of faith before becoming a full and conscious awareness of God's salvific plan for her. And here we have the starting point for the transforming action of grace in the soul of Elizabeth. Now is added to the personal effort involved in the integral development of her spiritual character, the penetrating, purifying action of the Holy Spirit.

In the process of the purification and growth of her life in God, Elizabeth passes through the spiritual phases designated by God's touch. Seeing and doing all things in the perspective of faith, motivated by a firm hope, and animated by a profound charity, she was able to cultivate a Christian and spiritual attitude that was so perfect that it was manifested externally in her relations with others. The gifts of the Holy Spirit and the three theological virtues were so evident in her that life became an epiphany of her pilgrimage towards the Absolute.

Through the dynamism of grace and the operation of the gifts of the Holy Spirit, Elizabeth penetrated the mystery of the triune God. Or, to put it in a better way, the Holy Spirit who acted within her was dwelling within her together with the Father and the Son to the point of taking complete possession of her. As a result, the young Carmelite was enabled to perform all her actions in a supernatural mode that is proper to the gifts of the Holy Spirit. Consequently, she was able to understand what it is to live in God simply by fixing her contemplative gaze on her own interior, where the Holy Spirit was operative.

Transforming Action

FIRMLY ANCHORED as she was in the divine mysteries, Elizabeth became more and more aware of the inner life of the Trinity that dwelt within her. She had become truly a child of God, in accordance with the teaching of St. Paul: "All who are led by the Spirit of God are children of God" (Rm 8:14). Her adoptive filiation and her sharing in the love of God are evidence of the dynamic but hidden operation of the Holy Spirit, who infuses and sustains new life, as Jesus taught:

> *I tell you most solemnly, unless a man is born through water and the Spirit, he cannot enter the kingdom of God: what is born of the flesh is flesh; what is born of the Spirit is spirit. Do not be surprised when I say: You must be born from above. The wind blows wherever it pleases; you hear its sound, but you cannot tell where it comes from or where it is going. That is how it is with all who are born of the Spirit (Jn 3:5-8).*

Every Christian life is necessarily related to the mystery of the incarnation as its source and origin, but the elevation to a new life is the immediate and personal work of the Holy Spirit, whom Elizabeth sees as a "devouring flame," that is, a flame of love that purifies and transforms into itself whatever it touches.

> *Our God, wrote St. Paul, is a consuming fire, that is a "fire of love" which destroys, which "transforms into itself everything that it touches." "The delights of the divine enkindling are renewed in our depths by an unremitting activity: the enkindling of love in a mutual and eternal satisfaction. It is a renewal that takes place at every moment in the bond of love."* [1]

Renewed in the Spirit, Elizabeth becomes a new creation and bears the distinctive marks of a *pneumatikos* (1 Cor 2:15). She is a spiritual being not only because her actions proceed from the Spirit, but also because she comports herself in such a way that, forgetting the works of the flesh, she renews herself daily (2 Cor 4:16) in the image of the Creator (Col 3:10). Effecting in her the mystery of rebirth (Tt 3:5), the Holy Spirit gives her a new mode of being that conforms to the image of the Son of God who dwells in her.

Elizabeth thus became an instrument in the hands of God and as she describes it, she remained "like a lyre under the mysterious touch of the Holy Spirit so that he may draw from it divine harmonies." [2] "In reality it is the Spirit of love and of strength who transforms the soul, for to him it has been given to supply what is lacking to the soul." [3] For Elizabeth's part, her progress along the path to sanctity was by means of the grace of interior purification, and as she progressed, she belonged more and more to God — as expressed by her religious consecration and her dedication to the praise of God. Ever conscious of the anointing of the Holy Spirit, who alone penetrates the abyss of God, she strove always to allow him to work in her the marvelous effects of his grace. Indeed, she would make of herself a "temple of God" (1 Cor 3:16) wherein she could celebrate divine worship "in accordance with the Spirit of God" (Ph 3:3), offering herself as a living, holy and acceptable victim. In other words, Elizabeth felt called to make of her entire life a liturgy of praise, which consisted in living in God's presence the sanctity infused in her soul by the Holy Spirit.

A life simplified to that extent, how much it resembles the life of the blessed! How detached it is from self and from all things else! "Everything is reduced to unity, to that 'one thing necessary' of which the Master spoke to Magdalene. Now the soul is truly great, truly free, because it has enclosed its will in that of God."[4]   In addition to that, Elizabeth received the grace of humble and trusting abandonment into the hands of the Beloved, a grace that she had requested through the intercession of Therese of Lisieux.[5]   She truly lived out the meaning of her name — temple of God — and through the indwelling of the Spirit of love she became one with him. Consequently, when speaking of her union with the Trinity, Elizabeth speaks repeatedly of "identity" or "identification," of "fusion" and "transformation into another you," of "passage into God" or "divine equality with God." She is here trying to express her divinization to the point of renewing in her soul the incarnation of the Word.[6]   In this way she contributes to the fulfillment of God's salvific plan, of which the Holy Spirit is the principal agent.

Her teacher in the school of the spiritual life is the Holy Spirit and, prompted and renewed by his transforming grace, she abandons herself in all things to her divine guide. Under the action of the Holy Spirit she penetrates the mystery of God and savors the divine presence through a contemplative intuition. In this mystical aura the Spirit of understanding and wisdom leads her to the "complete truth" (Jn 16:13): an intuitive understanding and mysterious fruition of God who is love.

The Holy Spirit And Elizabeth's Spiritual Growth

To LIVE IN and by the Holy Spirit meant for Elizabeth to act and to be sanctified no longer through human effort but by means of a divine operation. In the measure that she enters into the life of God under the guidance of the Holy Spirit and thus progresses in adoptive filiation, she becomes more and more detached from everything human.

> *Yes, we have become his through baptism; that is what Paul means by these words: "He called them" (Rm 8:30); yes, called to receive the seal of the Holy Trinity. At the same time we have been made, in the words of St. Peter, "sharers in the divine nature" (2 P 1:4); we have received "a beginning of his existence" (Heb 3:14).*[7]

Like every baptized person, Elizabeth had received, together with the sanctifying grace that gives a sharing in the divine life and nature, the infused supernatural virtues and the gifts of the Holy Spirit. And when these supernatural powers are operative, she becomes, as St. Thomas Aquinas says, a "sharer in the divine Word and in the Love proceeding."[8]   Consequently, the actions flowing from this participated divinity are likewise divine or, as St. Thomas says, they have a divine modality (*modo divino*).[9] This new — divine — manner of acting is the first fruit of the gifts of the Holy Spirit; it is one of the acts of love that the Trinity performed in Elizabeth's interior life.

The new mode of life and action that characterized the Carmelite of Dijon in the process of her "deification" was firmly rooted in the three theological virtues of faith, hope and charity. As regards the virtue of faith, Elizabeth writes as follows:

> *"To approach God we must believe" (Heb 11:6). Thus speaks St. Paul. He also says: "Faith is the substance of*

things to be hoped for, the evidence of things not seen" (Heb 11:1). That is, "faith makes so present and so certain the future goods that by it they take on existence in our soul and subsist there before we have fruition of them."[10] *St. John of the Cross says that it serves as "feet" to go "to God," and that it is "possession in an obscure manner." "It alone can give us true light" concerning him whom we love, and our soul must "choose it as the means to reach blessed union." "It pours out in torrents in the depths of our being all spiritual goods. Christ, speaking to the Samaritan woman, indicated faith when he promised to all those who would believe in him that he would give them a 'fountain of water springing up unto life everlasting.' " "Thus, even in this life faith gives us God, covered, it is true, with a veil but nonetheless God himself."*[11]

For the young Carmelite faith is a face-to-face encounter with God, but in darkness; it is a prelude to vision. Secondly, faith is a firm belief in God's love for us, accompanied by trusting and total abandonment.

"We have come to know and to believe in the love God has for us" (1 Jn 4:16). That is our great act of faith, the way to repay our God's love for love; it is the "mystery hidden" (Col 1:26) in the Father's heart, of which St. Paul speaks, which, at last we penetrate and our whole soul thrills!. . . It no longer rests in inclinations or feelings; it matters little to the soul whether it feels God or not, whether he sends it joy or suffering: it believes in his love. The more it is tried, the more its faith increases, because it passes over all obstacles, as it were, to go rest in the heart of infinite Love who can perform only works of love.[12]

This attitude of a lived faith in response to the proposal of salvific and crucifying love was necessarily accompanied by a firm hope that is able to hope against all human hope. While confidently waiting to attain to eternal Love beyond every veil, she lives in hope. This is one of the dynamic elements of her spiritual life: "We know that when he appears, we shall be like him, for we shall see him just as he is. And everyone who has this hope in him makes himself holy, *just as he himself is holy*" (1 Jn 3:2-3).[13] Although Elizabeth experiences herself as a daughter of God, she looks forward in hope to seeing him as he actually is, without any obscurity, in the life to come.

For Elizabeth, therefore, the virtue of hope is as it were an aspect of the virtue of faith and inseparably connected with the virtue of charity. Her charity was such that she loved God and neighbor to the point that she was willing to give her life for them. "Let us ask him to make us true in our hearts, that is, to make us sacrificial victims, for it seems to me that sacrifice is nothing else but love translated into action."[14] Hence, the three theological virtues and the seven gifts of the Holy Spirit were the spiritual faculties through which Elizabeth had a vivid experience of the divine. And, as we have seen, the theological virtues were closely interrelated. For Elizabeth there is no hope without faith and love for the Word. She believes and she loves because she has the hope of being transformed into his glorious likeness. Therefore, her hope sustains her faith and love, while they in turn stimulate and nourish the confidence of her hope.

In Elizabeth as in all the just, the sanctifying grace infused in her soul by the Holy Spirit is the soul of the supernatural organism of the infused virtues and the gifts of the Holy Spirit. As regards the gifts, their activity was noteworthy in her Carmelite life, though not all were operative to the same degree. Under the action of the Holy Spirit, the gift of fear of the Lord produced a detachment from everything that is not God, in order to take refuge in him alone. The gift of fortitude was especially evident in the courageous manner in which she endured suffering, desiring even at the age of nineteen to "live and die as one crucified."[15]   Through the gift of piety she directed all her love primarily to the one and triune God, endeavoring to offer to him the worship that is his due. Though perhaps less evident in her, through the gift of counsel she exercised complete docility to the promptings of the Holy Spirit and to the guidance of her lawful superiors. Finally, through the intellectual gifts of knowledge, understanding and wisdom Elizabeth was able to experience the emptiness of created things and the contingency of human existence in this world. On the other hand, she knew as it were intuitively and penetrated deeply into divine and eternal Truth, to which she was closely united in the heaven of her soul.

Thus we see that the ensemble of the gifts of the Holy Spirit was evident in the spiritual life of Elizabeth to a remarkable degree. As an authentic contemplative, she was borne aloft on the wings of the divine Eagle and was carried ultimately to that lofty sphere in which she experienced an intimate union with the triune God. There, "the Spirit of love, who seals and consummates the unity in the Trinity, pours himself abundantly upon her and bears her in the light of faith to those heights where life is only peace, love, union, lighted up even now by the rays of the divine Sun."[16]

The Holy Spirit And The Divine Indwelling

WORKING through the seven gifts, the Holy Spirit moved the will and intellect of Elizabeth in relation to her supernatural activity. Thus, under the influence of the gift of piety she was prompted to address God as Father.

> In heaven each soul is a praise of glory of the Father, the Word, and the Holy Spirit, for each soul is established in pure love and "lives no longer its own life, but the life of God." Then it knows him, St. Paul says, as it is known by him (1 Cor 13:12). In other words, "its intellect is the

intellect of God, its will the will of God, its love the very love of God. In reality it is the Spirit of love and of strength who transforms the soul.'' [17]

As an adopted child of God, Elizabeth can cry out from the depths of her soul: ''Abba, Father!'' The Holy Spirit himself ''gives witness with our spirit that we are children of God.'' (Rm 8:16).[18]   Without any fear of error she can affirm that through sanctifying grace and divine charity the three Persons of the Trinity dwell within her, and their presence becomes ever more intimate in the measure that she grows in grace and charity. She can indeed claim to be a temple of God in view of the teaching of St. Paul: ''Didn't you realize that you were God's temple and that the Spirit of God was living among you? If anybody should destroy the temple of God, God will destroy him, because the temple of God is sacred; and you are that temple'' (1 Cor 3:16-17). The holiness of that temple is established on the grace of humility, which draws the Holy Spirit to dwell in the soul.

The reality of the divine indwelling is likewise supported by her intense and faithful love, which was translated into works performed according to the precepts of the Lord:

''If anyone loves me, he will keep my word and my Father will love him, and we will come to him and make our home in him'' (Jn 14:23). The Master once more expresses his desire to dwell in us. ''If anyone loves me!'' It is love that attracts, that draws God to his creatures: not a sensible love but that love ''strong as death that deep waters cannot quench'' (Ep 1:18). [19]

The indwelling of the Trinity in the soul is thus identified with union through love, according to the statement of St. John, which Elizabeth makes her own: ''God is love and anyone who lives in love lives in God, and God lives in him'' (1 Jn 4:16). For Elizabeth there is no indwelling of the Trinity without the grace of God and the charity of the Holy Spirit. Charity, indeed, is especially appropriated to the Holy Spirit, but by reason of the circuminsession of the divine Persons in the one divine nature, it is attributed likewise to the Father and the Son.

> *If you read the Gospel according to St. John, you will see that our Lord constantly stresses this commandment: "Abide in me and I in you" (Jn 15:4). And again, you have that beautiful thought which I put at the beginning of my letter, in which he speaks of* making his abode in us *(Jn 14:23). In his Epistles, St. John desires that we should have* fellowship *with the most Holy Trinity. This expression is so sweet and simple. It is enough — St. Paul says so — to believe that God is a Spirit (Jn 4:24) and that we go to him by faith. Think of the fact that your soul is "the temple of God" (2 Cor 6:16). Again it is St. Paul who tells you so. At every moment of the day and night the three Persons are dwelling within you. You possess the sacred humanity only when you receive Holy Communion, but the divinity, that essence which the blessed adore in heaven, is in your soul.*[20]

In virtue of the divine indwelling, the soul of Elizabeth became the privileged locale of the triune God, the hidden heaven of her interior where she could adore her beloved Three. The coexistence of Father, Son and Holy Spirit in the Trinity, the reciprocal compenetration of Father and Son in the Spirit of love, and finally, the indwelling of the Holy Spirit in her soul constitute the central nucleus around which revolves and is structured the ascetical and mystical *pneumatology* of Elizabeth.

> *God in me; I in him: let this be our motto. What a joyous mystery is the presence of God within us, in this intimate sanctuary of our souls, where we can always find him even*

though we may have no sensible feeling of his presence. But
he is there, all the same. Perhaps he is even closer when we
feel his presence least. [21]

Recollected interiorly, her soul became an anticipated heaven in
which, even before the veil is removed, she enjoys the intimate
presence of the triune God.

On the mountain of Carmel, in silence, in solitude, in a
prayer that never ceases because it continues through all
else, the Carmelite lives as though already in heaven, by
God alone. The selfsame God who will one day be the cause
of her beatitude and will fully satisfy her in glory, is already
giving himself to her. He never leaves her; he dwells within
her soul; more than that, the two *become but one. . . She is*
identified with him whom she loves. . . There is the whole
Carmelite life: to live in him. [22]

To arrive at such a plenitude of life, Elizabeth generously exerted a
great ascetical effort and submitted herself to the purifying action
of the Holy Spirit. To live in the Spirit of God meant for her to be
sanctified during this period of vigil on earth and to experience the
presence of the divine Persons dwelling and operating within her
soul.

"If you knew the gift of God," Christ said one evening to the
Samaritan woman (Jn 4:10). But what is this gift of God if
not himself? And the beloved disciple tells us: "He came to
his own and his own did not accept him" (Jn 1:11). . . There
is one who knew this gift of God, one who did not lose one
particle of it, one who was so pure, so luminous that she
seemed to be the Light itself: "Speculum justitiae." One
whose life was so simple, so lost in God that there is hardly
anything we can say about it. . . She remained so little, so
recollected in God's presence, in the seclusion of the temple,
that she drew down upon herself the delight of the holy

*Trinity. . . the Father bending down to this beautiful crea-
ture, who was so unaware of her own beauty, willed that she
be the Mother in time of him whose Father he is in eternity.
Then the Spirit of love, who presides over all of God's
works, came upon her; the Virgin said her* fiat.[23]

Elizabeth also, like the Blessed Virgin Mary, mother and ideal
model, submitted to the operation of the Holy Spirit within her. She
assumed the selfsame attitude of the Virgin Mary, an attitude of
receptiveness, of silent adoration and of intimate union with her
Three, who took complete possession of her.

FOOTNOTES

1   Elizabeth of the Trinity, *Complete Works*, Vol. I, tr. A. Kane, O.C.D., ICS Publica-
    tions, Washington, D.C., p. 98. The quotations are from St. John of the Cross, *The
    Living Flame of Love*, Stanza 2, and from Ruysbroeck.
2   *Complete Works*, p. 112.
3   *Ibid.*, p. 111. This is an excerpt from St. John of the Cross, *Spiritual Canticle*, Stanza
    38.
4   Letter to Mlle. F. de Sourdon, October, 1906. Cf. Lk 10:42.
5   Cf. Letter to Mlle. G. de Remeaux, September, 1903.
6   In her prayer to the Trinity, Elizabeth asks the Holy Spirit: "Create in my soul a kind of
    incarnation of the Word." Cf. *Complete Works*, p. 183.
7   *Complete Works*, p. 105.
8   St. Thomas Aquinas, *Summa Theol.*, Ia, q. 38, a. 1.
9   St. Thomas Aquinas, *In III Sent.*, dist. 34, q. 1, a. 3.
10 A note in Elizabeth's *Manual* by Canon Gaume.
11 *Complete Works*, p. 101. The quotations are from St. John of the Cross, *Spiritual
    Canticle*, Stanza 12.
12 *Ibid.*, pp. 101-102.
13 *Ibid.*, p. 151.
14 Letter to Abbé Chevignard, December, 1905.
15 *Diary*, March 31, 1899.
16 Adaptation from a letter to Abbé Jaillet, February, 1902.
17 *Complete Works*, p. 111. The quotations are from St. John of the Cross, *Spiritual
    Canticle*, Stanzas 12 and 38.
18 *Complete Works*, p. 107.
19 *Ibid.*, pp. 96-97.
20 Letter to her mother, June, 1906.
21 Letter to Mlle. M. Gollot, April, 1901.
22 Letters to Mlle. G. de Gemeaux, August and September, 1902.
23 *Complete Works*, p. 110.

CHAPTER SIX

THE INDWELLING OF THE TRINITY

WHILE STILL a young girl, Elizabeth copied in her notebook a statement by St. Teresa of Avila: "You must seek me in yourself." Later, when she read *The Way of Perfection*, she came across the section in Chapter 28, where St. Teresa invites the reader "to retire into solitude in order to enter into oneself, to enclose oneself in the little heaven of the soul where he who created you dwells." This statement, which confirmed what Elizabeth had written as a child, caused Elizabeth to think a great deal as she was on the point of discerning her vocation in life: the indwelling of the Trinity in the heaven of her soul. A long and cordial conversation at Carmel with the Dominican, Father Vallée, not only clarified her ideas but convinced her of the vocation to which God had called her from all eternity.[1]

As a young Carmelite she never had any doubts; in Carmel she must live the indwelling of the Trinity because that is what she had been called to do. With the passing of time she penetrated ever more deeply into the mystery of the one and triune God, abiding in them after the Holy Spirit had prepared her soul to receive so great a gift.

When I think of it, my soul feels carried off by that great vision of the mystery of mysteries, of that Trinity which from now on is our cloister, our abode, the infinity in which we can transcend all things. I am now reading the beautiful pages of our blessed Father, St. John of the Cross concerning the transformation of the soul in the three divine Persons. To what an abyss of glory we are called! How well I understand the recollection and silence of the saints who could no longer leave their contemplation! That is how God was able to transport them to the divine heights where is consummated the union between him and the soul that has become his spouse in the mystical sense of the word. Our blessed Father says that then the Holy Spirit raises the soul to such lofty heights as to make it capable of producing in God the same spiration of love that the Father produces with the Son and the Son with the Father.[2]

If it is true that the Holy Spirit ushered Elizabeth into the divine sphere, it is likewise true that she does not lose her way along these paths but finds in the Word made flesh a model and guide with whom she identifies herself in order to plunge ever more deeply into the trinitarian mystery. The mystery of the indwelling of the Trinity that she experiences interiorly even in this life prompted her to strive to know as well as she could the theological and biblical aspects by which she could live fully the substantial reality.

She was successful in her quest, for she experienced the effects of mystical union of life with the Trinity. Completely forgetful of self, Elizabeth was made a sharer of the intimate life of God himself. The union was so profound that she was transformed or, to put it in her own words, she was divinized, deified. In this new state of life she experienced joy and peace alternating with suffering and aridity as the fruits of divine love. At these dizzy heights of Christian perfection Elizabeth was as it were lost in the ecstasy of God. She looked at, saw and judged earthly reality from a divine perspective. There was effected in her a simplicity of spirit that enabled her to look with a pure and simple gaze at the interior form of things and of all creation. She passed from ecstasy to a perception of the world with the limpid gaze of one who contemplates the face of God.

It may seem to the unwary that this chapter is a repetition of what we have already written. However, since it treats of the essential nucleus of the spirituality of Elizabeth of Dijon, it summarizes but does not simply repeat the themes previously treated. In this chapter we shall try to understand the mystery of the divine indwelling as experienced by our Carmelite mystic.

Doctrinal Foundation

ELIZABETH'S EXPERIENCE of the indwelling of the Trinity, which she lived profoundly, was based on Scripture and in addition on St. Thomas Aquinas (her early spiritual director was a Dominican), on St. Teresa of Avila, and especially on St. John of the Cross.

"I brought you to a fertile country to enjoy its produce and good things" (Jr 2:7). The words of the prophet Jeremiah apply very well to Elizabeth, who was called by name and led by the hand of the Son, through the power of the Holy Spirit, to rejoice in the marvelous perfection of the Father in his trinitarian mystery.

"We have been predestined by the decree of him who works all things according to the counsel of his will, so that we may be the praise of his glory" (Ep 1:11-12). It is St. Paul who announces to us this divine election, St. Paul who penetrated so deeply the "mystery hidden from eternity in the heart of God" (Ep 3:9). Then he gives us light on this vocation to which we are called. "God," he says, "chose us in him before creation that we might be holy and immaculate in his presence, in love" (Ep 1:4). If I compare these two explanations of the divine and eternal unchanging plan, I conclude from them that in order to fulfill worthily my work of Laudem Gloriae, *I must remain "in the presence of God" through everything; and that is not all: the apostle tells us "in love,"*

that is, in God, "God is love" (1 Jn 4:16); and it is contact with the divine Being that will make me "holy and immaculate" in his eyes.[3]

The foregoing quotation describes the manner in which the salvific plan of God was realized in Elizabeth. God predestined her; he called her by name; he inserted her in Christ; he made her a daughter of the Son and an heir of the perfections of the heavenly Father. Grafted on to Christ through baptism and her religious profession, she received, welcomed and experienced in the secret of her being, the transforming presence of the Holy Spirit. She was thereby elevated to a new mode of being: that of the praise of glory of the Trinity that she jealously guarded in her interior.

Made a sharer in the intratrinitarian mystery, Elizabeth becomes a new creation and recovers the pristine glory of God that daily permeates her more and more until she is transfigured and made conformable to the image of the Son in order to sing the praises of the Father for all eternity. She writes as follows on this point:

"Those whom God has foreknown, he has also predestined to become conformed to the image of his Son." And that is not all: "And those whom he has predestined, he has also called." Baptism has made you an adopted daughter and has signed you with the seal of the Holy Trinity. "And those whom he has called, he has also justified." How many times you have been justified through the sacrament of penance and those touches of God in your soul, of which you have not even been aware. "And those whom he has justified, he has also glorified." That is what awaits you in eternity, but remember that our degree of glory will be the degree of grace that God finds in us at the moment of our death. Let him complete in you the work of his predestination.[4]

Baptized in the blood of Jesus Christ, configured to his death and resurrection, signed with the seal of the Trinity, Elizabeth is placed under the guidance and influence of the Holy Spirit. In virtue of her adoptive filiation, she enters into communication with the reality of the Trinity, since filiation is the fruit of the Father's love and a free gift of the Spirit who asks her to be conformed to the image of the only-begotten Son (Rm 8:29). Thus is verified in her the statement of Isaiah: ''The glory of Lebanon is bestowed on it, the splendor of Carmel and Sharon. They shall see the glory of Yahweh, the splendor of our God'' (Is 35:2). Placed fully under the influence and service of the Trinity, Elizabeth savors in advance the eternal glorification that belongs by right to every child of God. This is the biblical nucleus, taken especially from St. Paul and St. John, that forms the basis for the spiritual doctrine of Elizabeth concerning the indwelling of the Trinity.

This doctrine is likewise corroborated by the teaching of St. Thomas Aquinas and the Spanish mystics. As regards the indwelling of the Trinity and sanctifying grace, St. Thomas writes:

> *There is one general way whereby, as the cause present in those that share in his goodness, God is in everything by his essence, power and presence. Over and above this there is a special presence consonant with the nature of an intelligent being, in whom God is said to be present as the known in the knower and the loved in the lover. And because by these acts of knowing and loving the intelligent being touches God himself, by reason of this special way of being present we have the teaching that God is not merely in the intelligent creature, but dwells there as in his temple. No other effect but sanctifying grace, then, is the explanation of a divine person's being present to the intelligent being in this new way.*

*Likewise the meaning of possessing something is that it is in
our power to use and enjoy it at will. To have the power to
rest joyfully in a divine person is ours by reason of grace
alone. Still, as grace is given the Holy Spirit himself is
possessed and dwells in a person and so it is he himself who
is given and sent. . . Admittedly, the effect of grace is also
from the Father, who abides in us through grace even as do
the Son and the Holy Spirit. . . The entire Trinity abides in
the soul by reason of sanctifying grace. "We will come to
him and take up our abode with him" (Jn 14:23).*[5]

St. Thomas Aquinas insists again and again that with the very
gift of sanctifying grace, the entire Trinity dwells in the souls of the
just. But that is not all. In his commentary on St. John's Gospel he
states further: "God's indwelling, whether by glory or by grace,
cannot be known except by experiencing it." And how does one
experience the indwelling Persons of the Trinity? Aquinas gives
the answer in his commentary on Second Corinthians when he says
that God is in all things as the cause that creates them and preserves
them in being, but he *dwells* in the souls of the just through
sanctifying grace and their own acts whereby they know and love
God, i.e., by faith and charity. The awareness of the divine
indwelling is, it should be noted, a "quasi-experiential"
knowledge, a loving knowledge; and the experience that follows
from this admits of varying degrees from the minimal or habitual to
the mystical experience of the transforming union.[6]

Following the example of St. Teresa of Avila, who repeatedly
speaks of the interior of the soul as the place where God dwells (cf.
The Interior Castle), and the example of St. John of the Cross,
defender of the transforming union attained in the most interior
point of one's being through the death and spoliation of self,
Elizabeth directed her entire life toward union with the divine
Persons in the silence and recollection of her soul.

A faithful follower of St. John of the Cross in the science of the *"nescivi,"*[7]   she passed through all the stages of death, spoliation and recollection to immerse herself in a union of love with her Three. In *The Ascent of Mount Carmel* the Mystical Doctor describes the nature of the initial union with God:

> *When we speak of union of the soul with God, we are not speaking of the substantial union that is always effected in creatures, but of the union and transformation of the soul with God . . . that comes from love; we shall therefore call this the union of likeness. . . The former is natural; the latter is supernatural. And the latter occurs when the two wills — that of the soul and that of God — are in total conformity and there is nothing in the one that is repugnant to the other. Thus, when the soul rids itself completely of that which is repugnant to the divine will or is not conformable to it, the soul becomes transformed in God through love. . .*
>
> *Wherefore, although it is true that God is always in the soul, giving it and by his presence preserving its natural existence, he does not always communicate supernatural existence to it. This is effected only by love and sanctifying grace, which not all souls possess; and of those who do possess it, they do not all possess it to the same degree. . . God communicates himself most to the soul that has progressed farthest in love; that is, the soul that has its will in closest conformity with the will of God. And the soul that has attained complete conformity and likeness to the divine will is totally united and transformed in God supernaturally.*[8]

If the soul progresses along this pathway of love, it will eventually attain to the spiritual marriage described by St. John of the Cross:

> *When this soul is so near to God that it is transformed in the flame of love, wherein the Father and the Son and the Holy*

Spirit commune with it, would it be incredible to say that it enjoys a foretaste of eternal life, although this cannot be to a perfect degree because the conditions of the present life do not allow it? Nevertheless the delight caused in the soul by that inflaming of the Holy Spirit is so sublime that it gives the soul a foretaste of the savor of eternal life.[9]

This is what was effected in the heart of the little ''praise of glory of the Trinity'' under the guidance of the revealed word and the teaching of the mystical theologians. In response to so great a grace, Elizabeth lived the mystery of the Trinity so intensely that she saw in it her mission in the Church, both in her lifetime and after her death. ''It seems to me that in heaven my mission will be to draw souls, by helping them to go out of themselves in order to adhere to God by a very simple, wholly loving movement and to maintain them in that great inner silence which allows God to imprint himself on them and to transform them into himself.''[10]

The Reality Of The Indwelling Of The Trinity

IT WOULD BE out of place to look for a rigorously systematic doctrine on the indwelling of the Trinity in the writings of Elizabeth of Dijon. Apart from her general theological formation, which was minimal and little developed, she never tried to present herself as a theologian and much less to write a textbook of theology. Yet, as a contemplative mystic she actually lived and experienced the most sublime dogma of Catholicism. In virtue of the sanctifying grace she received, which is a communication of the divine life and nature, she was able to perform acts that are proper to God himself, namely, she knew and loved God as he knows and loves himself, as the one and triune God. As a true daughter of God in the Son, she was mysteriously ushered into the sphere of the life of the Trinity, where the Father loves the Son with an infinite divine love, and vice versa. From this reciprocal love proceeds the Holy Spirit, and all three divine Persons dwell in her soul so that she can call God by the name of Father. In other words, through grace and in imitation of the Holy Spirit she was inserted into that ineffable exchange of love that flows between the Father and the Son. She had reached the state described by St. Thomas Aquinas, wherein she became ''a sharer in the divine Word and in the Love proceeding.''[11]   In his commentary on the *First Book of Sentences* St. Thomas Aquinas speaks more precisely about the configuration of the just soul with the Trinity:

> *Just as in the going forth of all things from their source the divine goodness is said to proceed upon creatures, insofar as a received likeness to it represents that goodness, so too in the return of the rational creature to God the significance of the processions of the divine Persons is present. This is called a ''sending'' because some received likeness has its model and origin in the relations proper to the Persons and thus represents them; e.g., the Holy Spirit's relation to the Father is one of Love and that of the Son is as the Word expressing the Father. Hence just as the Holy Spirit proceeds invisibly into the soul through the gift of love, so does the Son through the gift of wisdom, and thereby is manifested the Father, who is the ultimate end to whom we return. And since by reason of these gifts there is in us a likeness to that which is proper to the divine Persons, by reason of this new way of being, . . . the divine Persons are said to be in us insofar as we are made like them in a new way.[12]*

And so it was with Elizabeth. Her soul was elevated by divine grace to a loving contemplation that was marvelous and incessant, with the result that she was able to experience God as one and three, as an object of knowledge and love on the supernatural level.

*We carry our heaven within us, since he who completely
satisfies every longing of the glorified souls, in the light of
the beatific vision, is giving himself to us in faith and
mystery. It is the same thing. It seems to me that I have found
my heaven on earth, since heaven is God and God is in my
soul. The day I understood that, everything became clear to
me and I wish I could whisper this secret to those I love in
order that they also might cling closely to God through
everything, and that Christ's prayer might be fulfilled:
"Father, . . . that they may be made perfect in one."* [13]

Hence, the young Carmelite enters into herself so that with her
brethren she may be consumed in the love of the Trinity.

*"I must stay in your house." It is my Master who expresses
this desire! My Master who wants to dwell in me with the
Father and his Spirit of love, so that, in the words of the
beloved disciple, I may have "communion" with them (I Jn
1:3). "You are no longer guests or strangers, but you
already belong to the House of God," says St. Paul (Ep
2:19). This is how I understand "belong to the House of
God": it is in living in the bosom of the tranquil Trinity, in
my interior abyss, in this "invincible fortress of holy recollection" of which St. John of the Cross speaks.* [14]

Faith is essential to the life of communion with the Trinity because
it is the vehicle that brings the soul into the divine presence. "God
is spirit," says Elizabeth, "and it is by faith that we draw near to
him." [15]   In another place she expressed it as follows:

*If I want my interior city to have some similarity and likeness
to that of "the King of eternal ages"* [16]   *and to receive this
great illumination from God, I must extinguish every other
light and, as in the holy city, the Lamb must be "its only*

light.'' [17]   *Here faith, the beautiful light of faith appears. It
alone should light my way as I go to meet the Bridegroom. . .
"Faith," says St. Paul, "is the substance of things to be
hoped for, the evidence of things not seen."* [18]

*St. Paul says; "We are no longer strangers and foreigners
but fellow citizens with the saints and the domestics of God."
(Ep 2:19). We already live in the supernatural world by
faith. His love, his "exceeding charity," to quote the great
apostle again, there you have my vision on earth. Shall we
ever understand how greatly we are loved? To me, that
seems to be truly the knowledge of the saints.* [19]

It is through faith, therefore, that Elizabeth entered into the realm
of uncreated love and experienced the joy of realizing her vocation
fully. Thus, she wrote: "You see, there is a saying of St. Paul's that
is like a summing up of my life, and might be written of every
moment in it: 'For his exceeding charity.' [20]   Yes, all this flood of
graces is 'because he has loved me exceedingly.' ''[21]   The
overflowing and exceeding love of which Elizabeth speaks elicits
from her an existential response that is a mixture of joy and
suffering but eventually becomes a total giving and immolation of
her entire self as an answer to the appeals of God who is love. In
virtue of the divine love in which she shares, Elizabeth not only
enters into the sphere of the Trinity but she makes her own the
riches that she finds there. She immerses herself completely in the
Trinity by means of a profound faith and an exceeding love, with
her heart wide open to welcome the God who thus permeates her
life.

*I feel so much love upon my soul; it is like an ocean into
which I plunge and lose myself. It is my vision on earth,
while I await the vision face to face in the Light. He is in me
and I am in him. I have only to love him, to let myself be*

loved, at all times, in all circumstances. To awake in love, to
move in love, to sleep in love, my soul in his soul, my heart in
his Heart, that I may be purified and delivered from my
miseries by contact with him.[22]

The force of this exceeding love transported her out of herself into
the bosom of the Trinity in an ecstatic rapture. Immersed totally in
her Three, her life became a canticle of love of the divine perfections. And because she possessed in advance the mystical reality of
the Trinity, she experienced the virtue of hope as a diligent and
intense straining toward the beatific vision rather than a static
waiting for the mystery of God to be fulfilled in her.

Elizabeth's intimate experience of the Trinity was manifested
in her divine mode of thought and action and it effected in her soul
the phenomenon of the divine emissions. In fact, through the grace
of the divine indwelling the Persons of the Trinity were united to
her soul as the principle and norm of all her actions, which were no
longer human but divine in their modality. St. Thomas Aquinas has
stated that the Persons of the Trinity are given and possessed as
guiding principles of our return to God.[23]   In that regard Elizabeth
adds: "St. John of the Cross says that 'it is in the substance of the
soul, where neither the devil nor the world can reach,' that God
gives himself to it; then 'all its movements are divine, and although
they are from God, they also belong to the soul, because God works
them in it and with it.' "[24]   Finally, one should add that because
of their intimate union with the soul, the divine Persons are given as
an object of fruition and experienced love. All the mystics who
enjoyed this experience assert that they were aware of the presence
of the Trinity in their interior not only as an object of fruition that
they could enjoy with profound delight, but as a partner or spouse
on whom they could lavish all their love.[25]

Effects Of The Indwelling

IN DESCRIBING THE EXPERIENCE of the indwelling Trinity, Elizabeth not only gives evidence of God's presence within her, but she concentrates on the subsequent effects of the transforming dynamism of that presence.

> *It seems to me that the souls on earth and those glorified in the light of the beatific vision are very near to one another, since they all share in the communion of the same God, the same Father, who gives himself to the former in faith and mystery, and satisfies the latter with his divine glory. But he is the same, and we bear him within us. He inclines himself to us in all his love, day and night, in his longing to impart himself to us, to infuse his divine life into us, so as to make us deified beings, able to radiate him everywhere.*[26]

Consequently, the divine indwelling is not for Elizabeth a static reality but an exceedingly dynamic one; it is the source of the blessings bestowed on a soul possessed by God.

The first effect of divine love evident in Elizabeth is a total forgetfulness of self: complete detachment accompanied by a certain alienation that was no longer human but so ecstatic that she seemed to be no longer of this world. Thus, she wrote in a letter: "May his reign of love be then fully established in your interior kingdom, and may the weight of this love draw you to complete forgetfulness of self. . . Happy the soul that has attained this complete detachment. Such a soul loves truly."[27] The self-annihilation that the Holy Spirit worked in her with the hand of an artist, to fashion her in the image of the Son, was for Elizabeth a source of joy and lasting peace because it came from God.

> *Yes, I believe that the secret of peace and happiness is to forget oneself, to cease to be concerned with oneself. . . It*

*seems to me that the weakest soul — even if it is the most
guilty — is just the one that has the best grounds for hope,
and this act by which it forgets itself, to throw itself into the
arms of God, glorifies him more and gives him more joy than
all the falling back upon self, and all the self-examination
that makes it live in its wretchedness, while in its center it
possesses a Savior who comes at every moment to cleanse
it. . .*

*It may seem difficult to forget yourself; do not worry about it.
If you only knew how simple it is! I am going to tell you my
secret. Think about this God who dwells within you, whose
temple you are. It is St. Paul who says that,* [28] *so we may
believe it.* [29]

Elizabeth not only advised souls to strive for self-forgetfulness, but
above all she advised them to pray to God for the grace to be
detached from everything and everyone and to be his alone:

*Courage, then, Madame and dear sister; I am commending
you very especially to a little Carmelite who died at twenty-
four years of age, in the odor of sanctity, named Therese of
the Child Jesus. Before she died, she said she would spend
her heaven in doing good upon earth, and her grace is to
enlarge souls, to speed them forth on waves of love, confidence, abandonment. She said that she found happiness
when she began to forget self. Will you invoke her every day
with me, that she may obtain for you that knowledge which
makes saints, and gives so much peace and happiness to the
soul?* [30]

Like Therese of Lisieux, Elizabeth received an answer to her
prayer: to forget herself entirely and to be elevated by grace to the

supernatural state of trusting abandonment in the bosom of the
Trinity that she loved to the point of folly.

The grace of self-conquest was granted her in view of the
transforming union to which God had predestined her from all
eternity. As soon as the Holy Spirit gently drew her to himself,
detaching her from her own self, he began to introduce her gradually into the fellowship of the Trinity. As docile as an infant in the
arms of its mother, Elizabeth let herself be caught up in the vortex
of divine love.

> *Let us make ourselves small (like Sister Therese of the Child
> Jesus) and allow ourselves to be carried like an infant in the
> arms of its mother, by him who is our All. Yes, my sister, we
> are very weak; even more, we are nothing but wretchedness;
> but he knows that well and he so loves to forgive us, to lift us
> up, and then to carry us away in him, in his purity, in his
> divine sanctity. That is how he will purify us through con-
> tinual contact with him, by his divine touches. He wants us to
> be so pure. He himself will be our purity. We must allow
> ourselves to be transformed into a single image with him,
> and to do so with utter simplicity, loving at every instant with
> that love that establishes unity among those who love each
> other.*[31]

Called to live on such heights, Elizabeth yearned for nothing else
but to rejoice in God in the beatific vision throughout eternity, and
she was more than content to be granted a foretaste of it in this life.
" 'As the thirsty doe longs for the springs of fresh water, so my soul
longs for you, O my God! My soul thirsts for the living God! When
will I appear before his face?' And yet, as 'the sparrow has found a
home,' and 'the turtle-dove a nest in which she may lay her young,'
so *Laudem Gloriae* has found, while waiting to be brought to the
holy Jerusalem . . . her retreat, her beatitude, her anticipated
heaven in which she begins her life of eternity.' "[32] Rejoicing in the

mystical embrace of God, Elizabeth is drawn into the mystery of the Trinity and completely absorbed in the divinity of the three divine Persons, yet preserved her human nature with its sentiments of joy and suffering, toil and hope. The indwelling of the Trinity gives joy and peace, alternating with suffering and aridity; such was the intangible beatitude of Elizabeth, mystic of love. "It is the whole Trinity that dwells in the soul that loves them in truth; that is, by keeping their word. And when this soul has realized its riches, all the natural or supernatural joys that can come to it from creatures or from God himself are only an invitation to re-enter into itself in order to enjoy the substantial Good that it possesses, which is nothing else than God himself."[33]

It is characteristic of this new mode of being in God to experience joy and anguish at the same time: joy because the soul is in God's possession, but suffering because in the "game of love" God often hides from the soul. Hence, Elizabeth advises: "Do not attach too much importance to whether you are fervent or discouraged; it is the law of our exile to pass from one state to the other; but have faith that he never changes — that in his loving kindness he is ever bending over you, to carry you away and establish you in him."[34]   As to the rest, true glory — that which comes from God — is attained only through suffering. Elizabeth is so convinced of this that she can accept any kind of suffering and test of love in order to remain in intimate communion with her Beloved. She knows that "the soul visited by suffering abides in him."[35]

Because of her artistic rather than intellectual formation, her feelings had a great influence on her intellect, and yet, because of her deep immersion in the experience of the triune God, Elizabeth was able to leave self behind in order to be firmly established in divine contemplation. As a result, even in this life she lived in the hidden abyss of God. Living as she did beyond time but still behind the veil of eternal glory, she was on the one hand detached from everything in this world but on the other hand she manifested an

exceptional sensitivity, the result of a temperament inclined to seek
out the hidden meaning of things and the new state to which she had
been elevated. Anyone who, like Elizabeth, lives on a plane that is
no longer human but supernatural, perceives with a pure and
simple gaze the interior reality of things and not their external
aspect. In other words, the Carmelite of Dijon enjoyed that free
creativity that is proper to the *Spiritual Creator*: a profound intuition and harmonious synthesis of earthly reality. Shortly after
entering Carmel, she wrote to her mother: "Enjoy this beautiful
region, because nature leads to God. How I loved those mountains
that spoke to me of God, but believe me . . . the horizons of Carmel
are even more beautiful; they are horizons of the infinite God. In
God I find all the valleys, lakes and panoramas.''[36]   Prompted by
the creative touch of the Spirit, she intuitively understood and gave
expression to the beauty of creation and her experience of it:

> *Peaceful was the night and profound the silence,*
> *As my little boat glided through the waters of the sea. . .*
> *Then the waves suddenly rose up*
> *And wrecked my little boat:*
> *Thus the Holy Trinity absorbed me.*
> *I plunged into that abyss, that sweet refuge,*
> *As I am in the Infinite.*
> *And in the Infinite my soul breathes and is lulled to sleep,*
> *Living with its "Three" in eternity.*[37]

Possessed completely by God, Elizabeth had the gift of transforming into prayer whatever she thought or did for others. This is what
gave rise to her well-known *Prayer* (*Elevation*) *to the Trinity*,
which is a synthesis of her interior life and her spiritual message. It
is also a formal expression of what occurred mysteriously in her
interior: in a mystical embrace of love — because God is love —
she possesses the essence of all things in the infinite Being.
Through her union with God who is love, wherein she possesses the

All, as St. John of the Cross frequently states, Elizabeth arrived at a love for all creation that was very positive. And yet, in reaching this, she did not rest in the esthetic form but in the internal essence, which is much more important because it is in time a gift of self in order to make all creatures share in her happiness.

All the foregoing was effected in her as a result of her deification by the transforming action of the Holy Spirit, as St. John of the Cross teaches:

> *There would not be a true and total transformation if the soul were not transformed in the three Persons of the Most Holy Trinity in an open and manifest degree. . . In the transformation which the soul possesses in this life, the same spiration passes from God to the soul and from the soul to God with notable frequency and blissful love, though not in the open and manifest degree proper to the next life. . . One should not think it impossible that the soul be capable of so sublime an activity as this breathing in God, through participation as God breathes in her. For, granted that God favors her by union with the Most Blessed Trinity, in which she becomes deiform and God through participation, how could it be incredible that she also understand, know and love — or better, that this be done in her — in the Trinity, together with it, as does the Trinity itself! Yet God accomplishes this in the soul through communication and participation. This is transformation in the three Persons in power and wisdom and love, and thus the soul is like God through this transformation. He created her in his image and likeness that she might attain such resemblance.*[38]

——————————— FOOTNOTES ———————————

1 M.M. Philipon, O.P., *The Spiritual Doctrine of Sister Elizabeth of the Trinity*, tr. by a Benedictine of Stanbrook Abbey, Newman Press, Westminster, MD, 1961, p. 10.
2 Letter to Abbé Chevignard, November 28, 1903.
3 Elizabeth of the Trinity, *The Complete Works*, Vol. I, tr. A. Kane, O.C.D., ICS Publications, Washington, D.C., 1984, p. 143.
4 Letter to Mlle. F. de Sourdon, October, 1906. The scriptural quotations are from Rm 8:29-31.
5 St. Thomas Aquinas, *Summa Theologiae*, Ia, q. 43, art. 3; art. 4, ad 2; art. 5, corpus; Vol. 7, tr. T.C. O'Brien, McGraw-Hill, N.Y., 1976.
6 *Ibid.*, pp. 260-262.
7 *Complete Works*, p. 141.
8 St. John of the Cross, *The Ascent of Mount Carmel*, Book II, chap. 5, para. 3-4.
9 St. John of the Cross, *The Living Flame of Love*, Stanza I, para. 6.
10 Letter to Sister Marie-Odile, October, 1906.
11 St. Thomas Aquinas, *Summa Theologiae*, Ia, q. 38, a. 1.
12 St. Thomas Aquinas, *In I Sent.*, dist. 15, art. 4, a. 1.
13 Letter to Mme. de Sourdon, 1902. The scriptural quotation is from Jn 17:21-23.
14 Cf. St. John of the Cross, *Spiritual Canticle*, Stanza 40, para. 3. Cf. Lk 19:5.
15 Letter to her mother, May or June, 1906.
16 1 Tm 1:17.
17 Rv 21:23.
18 Heb 11:1. The quotation is from *Complete Works*, p. 145.
19 *Complete Works*, p. 109.
20 Ep 2:4.
21 Letter to her mother, June, 1906.
22 *Complete Works*, p. 64.
23 St. Thomas Aquinas, *In III Sent.*, dist. 25, 9, 2, a. 2, sol. 4.
24 *Complete Works*, p. 95.
25 Cf. St. John of the Cross, *The Living Flame of Love*, B, Stanza 1, para. 3.
26 Letter to Abbé Beaubis, June, 1904.
27 Letter to Mme. Angles, January, 1906.
28 1 Cor 3:17.
29 Letter to Mme. Angles, November, 1905.
30 Letter to Mme. Angles, November, 1905.
31 Letter to Mlle. G. de Gemeaux, August, 1903.
32 *Complete Works*, p. 161. Scripture references are Ps 41:1-2; Ps 83:3.
33 *Ibid.*, p. 154.
34 *Ibid.*, p. 75.
35 Letter to Mlle. Gout de Bizé, September, 1906.
36 Letter to her mother, August, 1901.
37 Poem no. 105 in Vol. III of *Complete Works*.
38 St. John of the Cross, *The Spiritual Canticle*, B, Stanza 39, para. 3-4, *The Collected Works of St. John of the Cross*, tr. K. Kavanaugh — O. Rodríguez, Doubleday, N.Y., and Nelson, London, 1964.

CHAPTER SEVEN

PRAISE OF GLORY

IN THE SCHOOL OF CARMEL Elizabeth perceived ever more clearly her specific vocation and her personal charism in the mystical body of Christ: to live in union with God interiorly, in the innermost core of her being, where the Trinity dwells, once she had achieved the unity of her ego. It is there that the young Carmelite establishes herself and lives on the wave of pure contemplation. On that divine plane, in a supernatural atmosphere and alone with God the Alone, she enjoyed a fruition of the divine perfections. The passage in Lamentations (3:28) — "To sit in solitude and silence when the Lord fastens it upon him" — she liked to translate as: "The soul sits in solitude and remains silent because it will rise above itself." And this is what was effected in the soul of Elizabeth. Through the silence of her mental and emotional faculties in the solitude of Carmel, keeping her heart quiet and ardently aspiring to the divine, her soul was elevated to an intimate union with God where, in an ecstasy of love, she understood her vocation as "Praise of Glory." Then, summoning her noblest sentiments, which had been purified by the action of the Holy Spirit, she praises, adores and glorifies her divine Three-in-One.

The intrinsic glory of the Trinity in which she shares through her profound contemplation of the God dwelling within her arouses in her a humble and ecstatic adoration. This simple and spontaneous reaction that springs from her heart as an ascension of her soul

towards God produces in her a verification of the encounter between the most perfect Being who is God and herself, a poor and
humble cloistered nun. Her awareness of this encounter and union,
however, rather than causing her to turn back and reflect on herself,
stimulated in her a sense of exultation that permeated her entire
being, to the point of transforming her into an eternal praise of
glory of the Blessed Trinity. So limpid and transparent was her
praise of glory that God was manifested in her as the God who is
love, who raised her to himself by his free gift of love.

The Meaning Of A Name

HER EXPERIENCE of the indwelling Trinity as a living in union with
the divine Persons clarified for Elizabeth her proper vocation: to be
the praise of glory of the Trinity. Such was the name and vocation
assigned to her from all eternity by the heavenly Father, and it is
likewise the ultimate goal of every Christian. Such a vocation
destined her to share in the communitarian life of the three Persons
of the Trinity, but it also demanded of her that she follow the
ascending path that leads from her existence as a creature *of* God to
the full self-realization of herself *in* God. And that is what constitutes God's *extrinsic* glory.

St. Augustine has defined glory as "*clara notitia cum laude*"
("clear notion with praise") when referring to the glory that
belongs to God, one and three. The Eternal Father has a perfect,
clear notion or concept of himself, and through that concept he
intellectually generates his Word, the Son, in whom are reflected
all the perfections of the Father. Then, from the reciprocal contemplative knowledge between the Father and the Son, the Holy Spirit
proceeds as indefinable and infinite Love. Supernatural
knowledge, immeasurable love and eternal praise constitute a
continual activity under the impulse of love within the Trinity, and
this in turn is the *intrinsic* glory of the Trinity.

Then, when the human person recognizes the divine perfections in themselves, in creation and in himself by participation, he gives *extrinsic* glory to the entire Trinity. And that giving of glory to God, as we have said, is the ultimate end and purpose of all creation.

> *"We have been predestined by the decree of him who works all things according to the counsel of his will, so that we may be* the praise of his glory."[1] *It is St. Paul who tells us this. St. Paul who was instructed by God himself. How do we realize this great dream of the Heart of our God, this immutable will for our souls? In a word, how do we correspond to our vocation and become perfect* Praises of Glory *of the Most Holy Trinity?*[2]

The secret for giving glory to God is to fulfill his only will, always, everywhere and in every way. As Elizabeth states in one of her letters:

> *Perhaps you will say to me: "How are we to glorify him?" It is very simple. Our Lord revealed the secret to us when he said: "My meat is to do the will of him who sent me." If you attach yourself . . . to the will of this adorable Master and look upon every suffering and every joy as coming directly from him, then your life will be one of continual communion with him. Everything will be a sacrament which gives you God. . . God can be found in all things, and in a sense these things are nothing else but an irradiation of his love. So that is the way to glorify him in those states of suffering and weakness that are so difficult to bear.*[2]

By conforming itself to the incarnate Word, says Elizabeth, the soul, "stripped and set free of self and of all else, can follow the Master to the mountain," to pray there with him in her soul "a prayer of God."[3]   Then, still through the divine Adorer, he who is the great praise of glory to the Father, she will "ceaselessly offer a sacrifice of praise, that is, the fruit of lips praising his name."[4]

The place where one celebrates the glory of God is one's own soul. No baptized person should fear to enter into himself but should advert to the fact that he is one musical note that is essential to the symphony that all creation plays to the glory of the Creator. " *'Coeli ennarrant gloriam Dei.'* This is what the heavens are proclaiming: the glory of God. Since my soul is a heaven in which I live while awaiting the 'heavenly Jerusalem,' this heaven too must sing the glory of the Eternal, *nothing* but the glory of the Eternal."[5]   Then, commenting on the words of the Psalmist — "Day to day passes on this message" — she states:

> *All God's lights, all his communications to my soul are this "day which passes on to day the message of his glory." "The command of the Lord is clear," sings the Psalmist, "enlightening the eye." Consequently my fidelity in corresponding with each of his decrees, with each of his interior commands, makes me live in his lights; it too is a "message which passes on his glory." But this is the sweet wonder: "Yahweh, he who looks at you is radiant!" exclaims the prophet. The soul that by the depth of its interior gaze contemplates its God through everything in that simplicity which sets it apart from all else is a radiant soul: it is "a day that passes on to day the message of his glory."[6]*

Having discovered the triune God in the depths of her being, Elizabeth contemplates him, shares in his glory, and participates in his interior perfections. Then, by her exterior life she makes known to others this message of God's glory that she experiences within herself.

In order that she may continue to glorify God after her brief

EFFICACIOUS NOVENA TO THE SACRED HEART OF JESUS

O my Jesus, You have said: "Truly I say to you, ask and it will be given you, seek and you will find, knock and it will be opened to you." Behold I knock, I seek and ask for the grace of....

Our Father, Hail Mary, Glory be, Sacred Heart of Jesus, I place all my trust in Thee.

O my Jesus, You have said: "Truly I say to you, if you ask anything of the Father in My name, He will give it to you." Behold, in Your name, I ask the Father for the grace of....

Our Father, Hail Mary, Glory be, Sacred Heart of Jesus, I place all my trust in Thee.

O my Jesus, You have said: "Truly I say to you, heaven and earth will pass away but My words will not pass away." Encouraged by Your infallible words I now ask for the grace of....

Our Father, Hail Mary, Glory be, Sacred Heart of Jesus, I place all my trust in Thee.

O Sacred Heart of Jesus, for Whom it is impossible not to have compassion on the afflicted, have pity on us miserable sinners and grant us the grace which we ask of You, through the Sorrowful and Immaculate Heart of Mary, Your tender Mother and ours. *Say the Hail, Holy Queen and add: St. Joseph, foster father of Jesus, pray for us.*

About this Prayer. This novena prayer was recited every day by Padre Pio for all those who asked his prayers. The faithful are invited to recite it daily, so as to be spiritually united with the prayer of Padre Pio.

About the Triumph of Mary. In a letter, Sister Lucia of Fatima wrote the following:

"About the other questions, if it will be convenient to insist in order to obtain the consecration of Russia... Intimately I have spoken to Our Lord about the subject and not too long ago I asked Him why He would not convert Russia without the Holy Father making that consecration. (He replied) 'Because I want My whole Church to acknowledge that consecration as a triumph of the Immaculate Heart of Mary so that it may extend its cult later on and put the devotion to the Immaculate Heart beside the devotion to My Sacred Heart.'"

Call 1-800-263-8160 for a **free** copy of *The Fatima Crusader* Magazine and local listings for the daily, worldwide radio broadcast *Heaven's Peace Plan* and TV program *Fatima: The Moment Has Come.*

THE INTERNATIONAL FATIMA ROSARY CRUSADE

In Canada: 452 Kraft Road, Fort Erie, ON L2A 4M7

In U.S.A: Route 30, Box 281, Constable, NY 12926

To re-order ask for leaflet #LF18

Printed in Canada

earthly existence, Elizabeth endeavors to conform herself to the Word, the Adorer and Glorifier of the Father who sums up in himself all creation. And the heavenly Father, who judges her love — or rather, the degree of Christocentric grace operative in and through her — grants her the degree of glory that corresponds to her conformity to Christ crucified. As she says: "We will be glorified in the measure in which we will have been conformed to the image of his divine Son."[7] The sole activity of all glorified souls will be to know and love God eternally in the mystical contemplation of his face.

The glorified have this repose of the abyss because they contemplate God in the simplicity of his essence. "They know him," says St. Paul again, "as they are known by him,"[8] *that is, by intuitive vision, a simple gaze; and that is why, the great Saint continues, "they are transformed from brightness to brightness into his very image by the power of His spirit";*[9] *then they are an unceasing praise of glory of the divine Being who contemplates in them his own splendor.*[10]

Through the power of the Holy Spirit dwelling within her Elizabeth receives, as does every baptized believer, the grace of divine filiation, so that the soul reflects as in a mirror the glory of the Word. In her also, as in all graced Christians, who abandon themselves to the Spirit of Christ to the point of being identified with his likeness, there is effected a progressive passage "from glory to glory," a gradual but continuous movement from light to light in contemplation and in the significance of the person of Jesus. Placed in this condition of being led to ever greater perfection, she hopes to see in the Son, through the mediation of the Holy Spirit, the face of the Father as it is in reality. At the same time, since she has become so completely identified with the Son, the Father reflects his own perfections in her. "Such was the Creator's dream; to be able to contemplate himself in his creature and see reflected there all his perfections, all his beauty, as through a pure and flawless crystal. Is not that a kind of extension of his own glory?"[11]

That is how Elizabeth realized the vocation signified by her name: Praise of Glory of the Trinity. She lived that name with ever increasing enthusiasm in each passing moment because by now she was no longer her own; she belonged completely and exclusively to God.

> *A praise of glory is a soul that lives in God, that loves him with a pure and disinterested love, without seeking itself in the sweetness of this love; that loves him beyond all his gifts and even though it would not have received anything from him, it desires the good of the Object thus loved. . . A praise of glory is a soul that gazes on God in faith and simplicity; it is a reflector of all that he is; it is like a bottomless abyss into which he can flow and expand; it is also like a crystal through which he can radiate and contemplate all his perfections and his own splendor. A soul which thus permits the divine Being to satisfy in itself his need to communicate "all that he has,"[12]   is in reality the praise of glory of all his gifts.*[13]

The experience of Elizabeth, so generously lived, is a restatement of the vocation of every Christian and the ultimate purpose of the entire created universe: the glorification of the triune God in the very core of their being.

Adoration

THE holy and undivided Trinity that Elizabeth accepted in faith and contemplated in and through love in the center of her being was the Object of adoration because the law of her generous love demanded it. Since the activity of the blessed in heaven is adoration, Elizabeth also felt compelled to pour forth an unceasing act of adoring love for all eternity.

And they do not rest day and night, saying, "Holy, holy, holy is the Lord God almighty; who was, and who is, and who will be for ages unending". . . And they fall down and worship him, and they cast down their crowns before the throne, saying, "Worthy are you, O Lord, to receive glory and honor and power." [14]

How can I imitate in the heaven of my soul this unceasing occupation of the blessed in the heaven of glory? How can I sustain this uninterrupted praise and adoration?. . . To be rooted and grounded in love: such, it seems to me, is the condition for worthily fulfilling its works as praise of glory. . . First of all, the soul should "fall down," should plunge into the abyss of its nothingness. . . Then it can "adore." Adoration, ah! That is a word from heaven! It seems to me it can be defined as the ecstasy of love. It is love overcome by the beauty, the strength, the immense grandeur of the Object loved, and it "falls down in a kind of faint" in an utterly profound silence, that silence of which David spoke when he exclaimed: "Silence is your praise!" [15] Yes, this is the most beautiful praise since it is sung eternally in the bosom of the tranquil Trinity; and it is also the "last effort of the soul that overflows and can say no more" (Lacordaire). [16]

Before the mystery of love which is the Trinity, Elizabeth did not remain fearful and in awe but, conscious of the infinite movement of the love of God, she desired to respond with a similar love, though finite and limited. It was precisely this limitation of her love that made her realize her condition as a creature and the infinity of

God, and yet she related with the Trinity in a manner of sweet familiarity. At the same time, she could not do other than prostrate herself before God in grateful adoration and joyful homage. Her intimate relation with God produced in her a response of love that was spontaneous, conscious and expressed with total abandonment and the gift of self.

In this attitude and response Elizabeth had an intuition of God whom she contemplated in the simplicity of his essence as the source of the perfections that are shared mystically but nonetheless really by his creatures. God is recognized in them as a pure act of love communicating himself for all eternity.

The soul, by the simplicity of the gaze which it fixes on its divine object, finds itself set apart from all that surrounds it, set apart also and above all from itself. Then it is resplendent with this "knowledge of the glory of God," of which the Apostle speaks, [17] *because it permits the divine Being to be reflected in it, "and all his attributes are communicated to it."* [18] *Truly this soul is the praise of glory of all his gifts; through everything, even the most commonplace acts, it sings the* canticum magnum, *the* canticum novum, [19] *and this canticle thrills God to his very depths.* [20]

Detached from her surroundings, because totally absorbed in the presence of God, Elizabeth was able to adore him in the interior of her soul as if in an eternal present.

"Be perfect as your heavenly Father is perfect." [21] *When my Master makes me understand these words in the depths of my soul, it seems to me that he is asking me to live like the Father "in an eternal present," "with no before, no after," but wholly in the unity of my being in this "eternal now."* [22] *What is this present? This is what David tells me: "They will adore him always because of himself."* [23]

> *This is the eternal present in which* Laudem Gloriae *must be established. But for her to be truly in this attitude of adoration, so that she can sing, "I will awake the dawn,"*[24] *she must also be able to say with St. Paul, "For love of him I have forfeited everything."*[25] *... Then she "will adore her God always because of himself" and will live, like him, in that eternal present where he lives.*[26]

Totally detached from self, aware of her creaturely existence, and conformed to the example of the Eternal Word, Elizabeth discovered the fundamental secret of Christian living: adoration of the transcendent God not only in the fleeting moment of the present but in the eternal now that embraces this earthly existence.

The adoration of which Elizabeth speaks, sustained by faith and entered into in faith and not vision, was a movement of her entire being that was united with Christ. Indeed, it was through his sacred humanity that she was able to reach the Father.

> *Let us adore him in "spirit," that is, with our hearts and our thoughts fixed on him, and our mind filled with his knowledge imparted by the light of faith. Let us adore him in "truth", that is, by our works, for it is above all by our actions that we show we are true: this is to do always what is pleasing to the Father whose children we are. And finally, let us "adore in spirit and in truth," that is,* through *Jesus Christ and with Jesus Christ, for he alone is the true Adorer in spirit and truth.*[27]

With full realization of her vocation to divine perfection, in conformity with the obedient Christ, Elizabeth strove to fulfill the will of the Father in every way that she could. By her act of perfect docility to the divine will that she adored and with an experiential knowledge of God through her deep faith, she endeavored always to do what pleases him in her daily life. Moreover, like every

Carmelite, Elizabeth was expected to make her life an unceasing adoration of love of the divine Persons.

A Carmelite is a soul ever adoring
And obedient to God.
Everything tends to union with God,
Her heart raised on high and her eyes fixed on heaven.
She has found the one thing necessary,
Love and light: the divine Essence!
Absorbed in the world of prayer,
She becomes a true apostle.[28]

The awareness of being in her Carmelite vocation the praise of glory of the Trinity infused into her life of prayer and into her every contact with God the stamp of a perpetual adoration, celebrated as a liturgical action through, with and in Christ for the glory of God and for the benefit of all mankind. "Now how do we *effectively* desire and will good to God if not in accomplishing his will, since this will orders everything for his greater glory? Thus, the soul must surrender itself to this will completely, passionately, so as to will nothing else but what God wills."[29]

In Elizabeth's mind adoration took on a new meaning. Besides being the spontaneous and conscious expression of her closeness to God, it was above all a total adherence of her entire being to the will of God. This was the norm of her existence and her Christian life.

Praise

AMONG the characteristic descriptions of Elizabeth's contemplative prayer one should also include that of praise, which is something similar to thanksgiving but essentially different. In her prayer of thanksgiving the mystic of Dijon is grateful to God for his gifts; in her prayer of praise, on the other hand, immersed as she was in God, she refers to God as he is in himself and she praises him for being God. In a word, she gives him thanks for his immense glory. "A praise of glory is one who is always giving thanks. Each of her acts, her movements, her thoughts, her aspirations, at the same time that they are rooting her more deeply in love, are like an echo of the eternal *Sanctus*."[30]

Although somewhat similar to adoration, which connotes silent prostration before the marvels of God, Elizabeth's prayer of praise was an exultant acclamation, a joyful canticle that celebrated God because he is the Lord of all creation and because all his actions are in conformity with his divine Essence. As praise of glory of the Trinity the Carmelite of Dijon speaks in the name of all creation to praise the Lord. In so doing she resembles the blessed in heaven as described in the Book of Revelation:

> *Then a voice came from the throne; it said: "Praise our God, you servants of his and all who, great or small, revere him." And I seemed to hear the voices of a huge crowd, like the sound of the ocean or the great roar of thunder, answering, "Alleluia! The reign of the Lord our God Almighty has begun; Let us be glad and joyful and give praise to God, because this is the time for the marriage of the Lamb."*[31]

Created anew in the Spirit and living in communion with the living God, Elizabeth's entire life now becomes a hymn of praise to the Trinity as she eagerly awaits the time when she will sing her song of love face to face in heaven.

> *In the heaven of her soul, the praise of glory has already begun her work of eternity. Her song is uninterrupted, for she is under the action of the Holy Spirit, who effects everything in her; and although she is not always aware of it, for the weakness of nature does not allow her to be established in God without distractions, she always sings, she always adores, for she has, so to speak, wholly passed into praise*

and love in her passion for the glory of her God. In the heaven of our soul let us be praises of glory of the Holy Trinity, praises of love of our Immaculate Mother. One day the veil will fall, we will be introduced into the eternal courts, and there we will sing in the bosom of infinite Love. And God will give us "the new name promised to the Victor." [32]   *What will it be? LAUDEM GLORIAE.* [33]

For Elizabeth, to praise meant above all to give glory to God, to glorify him for the immense intrinsic and extrinsic glory of the Trinity, which has been communicated to all creation.

Another and more genuine concept of the praise of God as evidenced in the life of Elizabeth is that of praise as an active contemplation that exalts the holiness of God as shared by the soul. In order to realize this type of praise, the young Carmelite endeavored to depart from self, to detach herself completely from self and be clothed in Christ — dead, risen and glorified — and to thrust herself with an impulse of unifying love into the active contemplation of the glories of the Trinity. This is achieved through the mediation of the incarnate Word because he is the eternal Praise of the Father.

So that I may personally realize this divine plan, it is again St. Paul who comes to my aid and who will himself draw up a rule of life for me. "Walk in Jesus Christ," he tells me, "be rooted in him, built up in him, strengthened in faith, growing more and more in him through thanksgiving." [34] . . .

He is that rock on which [the soul] is set high above self, the senses and nature, above consolations or sorrows, above all that is not him alone. And there is complete self-control, it overcomes self, it goes beyond self and all else as well. . .

*Finally, he wants me to "grow in Jesus Christ through
thanksgiving": for everything should end in this! "Father, I
thank you!"*[35] *My Master sang this in his soul and he
wants to hear the echo of it in mine! But I think that the "new
song" which will most charm and captivate my God is that of
a soul stripped and freed from self, one in whom he can
reflect all that he is, and do all that he wills. This soul
remains under his touch like a lyre, and all his gifts to it are
like so many strings which vibrate to sing, day and night, the
praise of his glory!*[36]

According to Elizabeth, therefore, the praise of God can be seen as
an act of sonorous contemplation, which is like a musical note
sounded by the breathing of the Holy Spirit in the Mystical Body as
a praise of glory to the Father. Her practice of praise of God always
proceeds from her loving intuition of the glory of God in the ambit
of the community of the three divine Persons.

Completely purified by the purging action of the Holy Spirit
and made a sharer in the divine perfections, Elizabeth reflected in
her interior the simplicity and transparency of God. "A praise of
glory is a soul that gazes on God in faith and simplicity; it is a
reflector of all that he is; it is like a bottomless abyss into which he
can flow and expand; it is also like a crystal through which he can
radiate and contemplate all his perfections and his own
splendor."[37] A soul that permits God to satisfy in her his need to
communicate all that he is, all that he has, is truly the praise of
glory of all his gifts. Mirrored in the soul, God recognizes his own
being in the act of communicating his life to humanity by way of
suffering; that is, he sees there the image of his suffering Son in his
supreme act of love. For that reason Elizabeth yearned to be
associated with Christ crucified in order to become a worthy praise
of glory.

David sang: "How shall I make a return to the Lord for all
the good he has done for me?" This: "I will take up the cup
of salvation." [38] *If I take up this cup crimsoned with the*
Blood of my Master and, in wholly joyous thanksgiving, I
mingle my blood with that of the holy Victim, it is in some
way made infinite and can give magnificent praise to the
Father. Then my suffering is "a message which passes on
the glory" of the Eternal. [39]

Only by being united with the paschal Christ could Elizabeth sing
the praises of God and hand on to posterity his glory. And this is an
authentic glory because it has passed through the cross. Moreover,
she could not be a perfect praise of glory unless at the same time she
offered herself to Christ, the Victim of expiation for the entire
human race. Thus, the mystic of Dijon gave glory to the Father,
adored him interiorly, and gave him praise by offering to him her
crucifying love in an unbloody but no less painful and purifying
manner. All of this took place in an atmosphere of intense prayer,
in an invisible but profound union through faith, and in a love that is
the bond of the communion of saints. While waiting to contemplate
God beyond the veil and beyond faith, she gives herself completely
to him through love. "Faith is so beautiful! It is heaven amidst the
darkness, but one day the veil will fall and we shall contemplate in
the light him whom we love. And while awaiting the 'Come' of the
Bridegroom, we must be totally dedicated, suffer for him, and
above all, love him very much." [40]   Such was the life of
Elizabeth: a praise of glory united to the Crucified in faith, hope
and charity.

————————— FOOTNOTES —————————

1 Ep 1:11-12.
2 Letter to Mme. Angles, January, 1906. Cf. Jn 4:34.
3 Cf. Lk 6:12.
4 Cf. Heb 13:15.
5 Elizabeth of the Trinity, *Complete Works*, Vol. I, tr. A. Kane, O.C.D., ICS Publications, Washington, D.C., 1984, p. 149. Cf. Ps 19:2.
6 *Ibid.*, p. 149. The Scripture references are Ps 19 and Ps 33.
7 *Ibid.*, p. 105.
8 1 Cor 13:12.
9 2 Cor 3:18.
10 *Complete Works*, pp. 143-144.
11 *Ibid.*, p. 144.
12 Cf. St. John of the Cross, *The Living Flame of Love*, Stanza III, para. 1; also found in the writing of Ruysbroeck.
13 *Complete Works*, p. 112.
14 Rv 4:8, 10-11.
15 Ps 65:1.
17 *Complete Works*, p. 150.
17 2 Cor 4:6.
18 Cf. *Living Flame of Love*, Stanza III, para. 77.
19 1 Cor 13:12; Rv 14:3.
20 *Complete Works*, p. 144.
21 Mt 5:48.
22 Phrases are taken from the writings of Ruysbroeck.
23 Ps 71:15.
24 Ps 56:9.
25 Ph 3:8.
26 *Complete Works*, pp. 152-153.
27 *Ibid.*, p. 108.
28 *Ibid.*, Vol. III, poem no. 81.
29 *Complete Works*, p. 112.
30 *Ibid.*, p.112.
31 Rv 19:5-7.
32 Rv 2:17.
33 *Complete Works*, pp. 112-113.
34 Col 2:6-7.
35 Jn 11:41.
36 *Complete Works*, pp. 156-158, *passim.*
37 *Ibid.*, p. 112.
38 Ps 115:3-4.
39 *Complete Works*, p. 149.
40 Letter to Mlle. Rolland, April, 1903.

CHAPTER EIGHT

IN THE SERVICE OF THE CHURCH

"YOU YOURSELVES have seen what I did with the Egyptians, how I carried you on eagle's wings and brought you to myself" (Ex 19:4). The symbol of the eagle, so dear to Elizabeth, represents Christ, who carries the souls chosen by the Father on the wings of prayer and the cross. The mystic of Dijon also, borne on those wings to intimate union with God, relates with the divine Persons and her brethren in an entirely new way. However, in order to attain that union and encounter with God, she had to depart completely from self.

St. John of the Cross says that "it is in the substance of the soul, where neither the devil nor the world can reach," that God gives himself to it; then "all its movements are divine, and although they are from God, they also belong to the soul, because God works them in it and with it." [1]

The same saint also says that "God is the center of the soul." So when the soul "with all its strength will know God perfectly, love and enjoy him fully, then it will have reached the deepest center that can be attained in him." Before attaining this, the soul is already "in God who is its center," but it is not yet in its deepest center, for it can still go further. Since love is what unites us to God, the more intense this love is, the more deeply the soul enters into God and the more it is centered in him. When it possesses even one degree of love it

is already in its center; but when this love has attained its
perfection, the soul will have penetrated into its deepest
center. There it will be transformed to the point of becoming
very like God.[2]

At this stage of the spiritual journey, Elizabeth lived her charism as
a Carmelite to the fullest degree: called to intimate union with God
through her total gift of self, exactly as priest and victim mystically
offered in union with the paschal Christ. While experiencing the
triune God in contemplative prayer, Elizabeth intuitively under-
stands the essence of fraternal charity, which is in no way separated
from the divine love in which she has been made a participant.

Contemplative Experience In Carmel

THE CONTEMPLATIVE SERVICE of Carmel in a restless and
materialistic world flows from the very nature of the Carmelite
mystique, which is essentially a contemplative experience of God
through silent prayer and renunciation, in an atmosphere of solitude and total detachment. Prayer is seen as a communication of
love with God who is love, and it occupies a central place in
Carmelite life. Such a relationship that is founded on love should
be above all a giving of self to God and to neighbor, in accordance
with the twofold precept of charity. Consequently, the stages of
Carmelite prayer are designated according to the various degrees of
love and immolation. The point of departure is the certitude of
being loved by God with an infinite and merciful love; the terminus
is a response to love that scales the walls of the cloister, passes
beyond the confines of one's own interior, and expands in great
respiration of love to take upon oneself — in silence and solitude,
in suffering and immolation — the joys and the problems of all
mankind.

In accordance with the ascetical tradition of Carmel, in order to
experience God in contemplative prayer, Elizabeth had to place

herself in an attitude of silence and purity of heart. These are indispensable conditions for seeing and hearing God through the veil of this mortal life. Led by the Holy Spirit to contemplate the vivifying presence of God one and three, the young Carmelite gladly accepted the gift of contemplation, not to keep it for herself but also to give it to others. In this way, through suffering and solitude, she could become an adoring witness to the sanctity and love of God. "There is the whole Carmelite life: to live in him. Then all the sacrifices, all the immolations become divine. The soul sees him whom she loves through everything, and everything takes her to him. It is a continual heart to heart union." But this is followed by a horizontal movement towards one's neighbor: "A Carmelite ought to be apostolic; all her prayers and all her sacrifices are directed to this."[3]

The more she perceives God as the mystery of redemptive love to which mankind refuses to respond, the more she begs to embrace the cross together with Christ in order to be with him a victim of expiation and salvation. As early as 1899 she had written in her diary:

> *Since he is in me, lives in me, I shall speak to him in the secret of my heart; I shall bring him new sacrifices that will show him how much I love him and how much I desire to suffer and make expiation with him. O Jesus, my love, my life, my beloved spouse, your cross! I beg you, give me your cross. I want to carry it together with you. You have suffered enough for me; I want to console you. I am weighed down with the sins of the world. Don't look at anyone but me; don't strike anyone but me. I am your victim, as I am also your spouse and the confidant of your Heart.*[4]

To remain faithful to her vocation as victim and spouse, Elizabeth did not refuse any kind of suffering. The redemptive love that permeated her being necessarily produced in her an attitude of that kind. That same redemptive love was able to gather together all the anxieties and problems of mankind so that they could be rectified by the touch of God. Such was the apostolic zeal that came forth from her deep ecclesial sense; she yearned ardently for the glory of God and the salvation of the world.

We must be zealous for the salvation of our brethren. . . This zeal can be exercised in four ways: 1) By prayer. . . 2) By a good word. . . 3) By good example. . . 4) By sacrifice.

Jesus gained our redemption through suffering. He asks us to follow in his footsteps along the path of sacrifice; this is the most secure ransom for the salvation of souls. What else do I ask of you, Jesus, except suffering? I want to endure everything; I am ready to suffer everything, but give me the strength to do so.[5]

Elizabeth's life, like her prayer, was all love, a love that prompted in her an intense concern for God and neighbor. In her rapt attention to God she also became aware of others with their joys and their difficulties. And for this reason the mystic yearned for union with God, impelled by the needs of her sinful brethren, so that she could redeem them by her bloodless martyrdom in Carmel. In her dialogue with God there is effected in her an identification with all humanity, of whom she feels herself to be the representative and, in fact, she experiences the concrete apostolic effectiveness of her life in God. In other words, the mystical love that Elizabeth experienced in her encounter with God overflowed and reached her neighbor, to carry him to the vortex of the salvific love of God who is Love.

Since our Lord dwells in our souls, his prayer is ours. I wish to share in it constantly, to keep myself as a little jug at the spring, at the fountain of life, in order that I may be able

subsequently to give him to souls, by permitting the waters of
his charity to overflow. "For their sake I consecrate myself
so that they too may be consecrated in truth." [6]   *Let us*
make these words of our adorable Master entirely our own.
Yes, let us sanctify ourselves for souls and since we are all
members of the one body to the extent that we possess the
divine life, we can communicate it and diffuse it in the great
body of the Church. [7]

Elizabeth realized her Carmelite vocation in the Church by being a
"contemplative in action." And this was fully in keeping with
what St. Teresa of Avila had asked of her nuns: "It breaks my heart
to see so many souls traveling to perdition. I would the evil were
not so great and I did not see more being lost every day. Oh, my
sisters in Christ! Help me to entreat this of the Lord, who has
brought you together here for that very purpose. This is your
vocation; this must be your business; these must be your desires;
these your tears; these your petitions. . . If your prayers and desires
and disciplines and fasts are not performed for the intentions of
which I have spoken, reflect [and believe] that you are not carrying
out the work or fulfilling the object for which the Lord has brought
you here." [8]   Elizabeth paraphrased the teaching of St. Teresa as
follows: "As a true daughter of St. Teresa I wish to be an apostle in
order to give the greatest possible glory to him whom I love. Like
my holy Mother, I think that he has placed me on earth to work
zealously for his honor as his true spouse." [9]   And, we may add,
the desires of the spouse should not be contrary to those of the
bridegroom! Therefore, her apostolic desires were effectively
pursued within the context of and in conformity with her vocation
as a Carmelite: a vocation to love in a life of prayer.

The Carmelite has found the unum necessarium: *God, light,*
love; and when she encloses the world in her prayer, she is
truly an apostle. [10]

Such is the dynamism of Elizabeth's contemplative life. The triune God dwells in her but we may also say that in a certain sense God again becomes incarnate in her so that through her and in her he can continue to love mankind, redeemed by the precious Blood of his Son, through the power of the Holy Spirit. And the prayer of Elizabeth, in whom the Trinity is active, becomes fruitful precisely because it is prayer in the name of the Father and of the Son and of the Holy Spirit. As she had written to a friend: "Prayer does not mean binding ourselves to recite a certain number of vocal prayers daily, but the raising of the soul to God through all circumstances, which establishes us in a kind of continual communion with the Most Holy Trinity, quite simply by doing everything in its sight."[11]

Carmelite And Priest

ONE CANNOT UNDERSTAND the mystical life of Elizabeth unless it is seen as an unceasing intimate colloquy with the three divine Persons, and then a knowledge of the Other, the absolute of God, in which, through loving contemplation, she again seeks to find herself and her brethren who are burdened with cares and expectations. Rich in divine love and weighed down with the burdens of her brethren, Elizabeth spent her life in a total giving of self. Like a lamp burning before the tabernacle, she was consumed in an unceasing act of love, in solitude and silence, in sacrifice and self-immolation — the powerful means of intercession that attract the glance of God on the Church, on priests especially, and on all her neighbors, whether near or far.

Elizabeth felt herself responsible for the salvation of others, so she immersed herself in communion with God in solitude in order to pray better and, paradoxically, to be more open to the needs of others. Her mission was, above all, a sweet conversation with God for the good of her neighbors, imploring their redemption. While faithfully listening to the voice of the Spirit on the heights of contemplation, Elizabeth was ever attentive to all the voices that rise up from the earth, whether in prayer or not, voices that expressed joy or sorrow, comfort or fatigue, anxiety or hope. She accepted and embraced the daily life of every person with a salvific and liberating embrace in the charity of her prayer. As a result, her mystical life was an exquisite and prudent service of love for her neighbor, and for that reason she strongly emphasized the ministerial aspect of the cloistered life. The Carmelite charism and the priestly office are united at the heart of her mysticism because both spring from the same divine source for the benefit of all mankind.

How we feel the need of sanctifying ourselves, of forgetting ourselves, in order to be wholly occupied with the Church's interests. . . What a sublime mission the Carmelite has! She ought to be a mediator with Jesus Christ, to be another humanity for him in which he may perpetuate his life of reparation and sacrifice, of praise and adoration.[12]

It was in this blending of Carmelite and priest that Elizabeth understood her sublime vocation in Carmel: to work for the redemption of mankind in, with and through Christ. She often returned to this intimate relationship with Christ in order to give expression not only to her own pious aspiration but to the reality that she lived in her daily life.

Your mother's heart should feel a divine joy when you think that the Master has deigned to choose your daughter, the fruit of your womb, to be associated with his great work of redemption, in order that he may suffer in her, as it were, an extension of his Passion. The bride belongs to the Bridegroom. Mine has taken me. He wishes me to be another humanity in which he can still suffer for his Father's glory, to help the needs of his Church.[13]

The goal of this intimate association with Christ was unique and sublime: to be an instrument for the salvation of mankind. The only difference was that whereas the priest is a channel of salvation through the administration of the sacraments, she, like Magdalene, was a priest in the silent adoration of the Word. "The life of a priest, like that of a Carmelite, is an Advent that prepares for the Incarnation in souls."[14]   Both of them prepare and actuate — mystically but no less really — the presence of God in the souls whom they serve. It is, to be sure, a preparatory work but nonetheless meritorious and effective. And in both cases it calls for a total giving of self for the coming of the kingdom of God in the hearts of men.

Elizabeth lived her apostolic mission not only in her contemplation of God but also in her religious consecration and her daily participation in the Eucharistic Sacrifice.

Tomorrow is the feast of St. Mary Magdalene. . . It is also a feast for my soul, for on that day I keep the anniversary of my baptism. Since you are the priest of love, I come to ask you, with Reverend Mother's permission, to be kind enough to consecrate me to him tomorrow in Holy Mass. Baptize me in the Blood of the Lamb so that, utterly untouched by everything that is not he, I may live only to love him more and more passionately until I reach that happy unity to which God has predestined us in his eternal and unchangeable will.[15]

Elizabeth sees herself as spouse, victim and priest in the bosom of the mystical body of the Church; she thinks of herself as consecrated to those offices by her "priest-prioress." In the last days of October, 1906, Elizabeth refers to her prioress, Mother Germaine, as "my Holy Priest,"[16]   and in view of her consecration to a special vocation, she feels that she also is in some sense a priest: "And I understand also that in heaven I will fulfill in my turn a priesthood over your soul.''[17]   She sees herself, in a sense, as a sacrament of the love of God, a visible sign of the salvific presence of God for souls through her life as a Carmelite and priest.

Consequently, the contemplative life of Elizabeth was not confined within the walls of the cloister, but by reason of her interior dynamism it flowed out to the militant Church to bring salvation and holiness to all mankind. Because the mystic of Dijon was immersed in the Heart of Christ and could draw upon his own salvific love, she knew that her prayer was co-redemptive, like that of the Virgin Mary. Her life was an unbroken dialogue with God, lived in the silence and recollection of her own little Nazareth, and very little was visible externally. Nevertheless, it was most effective in touching the entire world, beyond the limits of time and place. Through and with the Virgin of contemplation, our little Carmelite was in her own way also a mediatrix with Christ the Savior, as she herself liked to say. Faithful to her role as mother and spouse, virgin and priest, she prayed and gave herself completely and prayed that all priests would be worthy of their sacerdotal ministry.

Fraternal Charity As A Contemplative Experience

INTRODUCED to the *koinonia* of the Trinity, Elizabeth received from the Holy Spirit the ability to know and love the Lord in her neighbors and to communicate with them in an entirely new and original manner. The love with which she loved them was a divine love, the expression of her intimate relationship with God. She was so pneumatic that she could contemplate the triune God in the neighbor whom she could not see but sensed as very close. To put it in another way, she made her own the salvific sentiments which Christ experienced for mankind. Abiding in the love that is God and is at the same time a gift from God, she was endowed with the selfsame power of divine love.

I would like to be completely silent and in adoration so that I could penetrate ever more in him and be so filled with him that through my prayers I could give him to those poor souls who do not know the gift of God.[18]

Sharing as she did with the paschal Christ in the intratrinitarian mystery, she exercised the selfsame apostolate of the love of God through her life as a contemplative Carmelite. Such was the apostolic character of her love as a contemplative, whereby she consecrated and offered herself completely to God and in him, to the service of her brethren. Charity, for Elizabeth, meant not only the generous apostolic service of a contemplative, but it was a vehicle of the divine love present in the Word incarnate, to whom she was totally assimilated.

O my Sister, to be identified with him; that is my whole dream. Don't you believe that even now a glance or a desire can become a powerful prayer that the Father, who contemplates his adored Son in us, cannot resist? O yes! We are identified with him and we go to the Father under the motion of his divine love.[19]

Since charity for Elizabeth was an experienced mystical union with God who is Love, she was able to contemplate God in an ecclesial context; that is, it brought her close to both God and neighbor; it was salvific because identified with the paschal Christ; and it raised her to the level of Christ, the universal Brother, because she shared in the saving power of Christ. It is in this context that she became a living prayer of petition for others and, we may say, a co-redemptrix in the salvific plan of the Father. She loved to repeat with St. Paul that those who are predestined to be conformed to the image of the Son (Rm 8:29), crucified through love, are those whom God has willed to associate with himself in the work of redemption. Rightly, then, did she apply to herself the title "mother of souls," in imitation of Mary, Virgin and Mother of a new humanity.[20] Such spiritual motherhood is as fruitful as the degree of one's love of God and neighbor.

Elizabeth's apostolic service flowed from the fecundity of her love which, in turn, was measured by the grace of God she had received. And grace was given her precisely in view of her hidden apostolic service rendered to God as praise of glory and to her neighbors as a co-redemptive irradiation. She became holy as a result of exercising that service in its twofold aspect. No longer living for herself, but absorbed into the mystery of intratrinitarian love, she relived the charity of God the Father, Son and Holy Spirit in relation to the world from which she was separated. "He has loved me and has given himself for me." Such is the terminus of love: self-giving, losing oneself completely in the one who is loved. "Love makes one go out from self to the one who is loved, in order to transport oneself by an ineffable ecstasy to the object of one's love."[21]

From the moment that Elizabeth was drawn into the charity of Christ, incarnate for the benefit of mankind, she was aware of her solidarity with the mystical body. "It is infinite Love which envelops the soul, and wills, even here, to associate it with all its blessings. The soul knows experimentally that the Trinity is living within it, the Trinity it will behold in heaven. . . I am Elizabeth of the Trinity, that is to say, Elizabeth disappearing, losing herself, letting herself be completely possessed by the 'Three.' This is the divine bond that unites us to the point of being one thing."[22]

Offering herself as a "victim of love" for the salvation of souls, the young Carmelite experienced a trusting abandonment in the bosom of the Trinity, in union with the pilgrim Church amidst the difficulties and anxieties of the present time. In this way she showed that the activities of Martha and Mary are not mutually exclusive but form a unity that is all the more effective and fruitful as Elizabeth was more faithful to her charism as a contemplative. Her dedicated love to the triune God was for her also a loving service directed to the salvation of souls. One can therefore say that Elizabeth's contemplative life had a reason for existing only with and in the Church, and precisely because the Church is the mystical body of Christ. Within this spiritual framework, while faithful to the Carmelite traditions, she performed the function of a heart that loves, suffers, groans and palpitates in unison with the Heart of Christ and then stretches forth to others with salvific aspirations. There was an invisible relationship and a marvelous compenetration between her absorption in the inner life of the Trinity and her increasing loving awareness of the Church that labors for the salvation of souls and the glorification of God.

As for St. Therese of Lisieux, so also for Elizabeth of Dijon, her vocation in the Church was to love without reserve. This love, which was to be her cloister and her program of life, will last throughout eternity because it is the only means by which she can enjoy God forever in heaven.

> *Yes, my little sister, I think it is love that does not permit us to remain for a long time on this earth. I believe — and St. John of the Cross expressly says so — that it is love which shortens our stay here on earth. There is a wonderful chapter in which he describes the death of souls who are victims of love: there are the last assaults of love, then all the rivers of the soul, which are already so immense as to seem like seas, lose themselves in the ocean of divine Love. . . If by a simple, loving gaze of faith we remain ever united to him and if, like our beloved Master, we can say, "I do always the things that please him,"*[23] *he will be able to consume us, and we shall be lost in the immense fire, to burn there at our ease for all eternity.*[24]

Only a love like Elizabeth's could reach such a lofty degree of intimacy with God that it enjoys already in this life a foretaste of the happiness of union with God that is proper to the life to come. Such is the goal to which the love between Elizabeth and the Trinity leads; and hers was a steady progress toward the coveted reality of a completely spiritualized heart in which the deifying union between the soul and God can come to full fruition. Everything between the finite human creature and the infinite Other disappears, according to the action of the Holy Spirit, who breathes where he wills and directs the soul how and where he pleases. And in the vortex of divine love Elizabeth did not run the risk of losing her identity or proper existence; rather, she was able to embrace all creation and make of it an eternal canticle of love to her adored Spouse.

─────────────────── FOOTNOTES ───────────────────

1 *The Living Flame of Love*, Stanza 1, para. 9.
2 Elizabeth of the Trinity, *Complete Works*, tr. A. Kane, O.C.D., Vol. I, ICS Publications, Washington, D.C., 1984, pp. 95-96. The quotations are taken from *The Living Flame of Love*, Stanza 1, para. 13.
3 Letter to Mlle. G. de Gemeaux, September, 1902.
4 *Diary*, February 10, 1899.
5 *Ibid.*, March 12, 1899.
6 Jn 17:19.
7 Letter to Abbé Chevignard, December, 1904.
8 St. Teresa, *The Way of Perfection*, tr. E. Allison Peers, Image Books, Garden City, N.Y., 1964, chap. 1, p. 38; Chap. 3, p. 51.
9 Letter to Mme. Hallo, May, 1906.
10 *Souvenirs*, p. 306.
11 Letter to Mlle. G. de Gemeaux, February, 1905.
12 Letter to Canon Angles, January, 1906.
13 Letter to her mother, September, 1906.
14 Letter to Abbé Chevignard, December, 1905.
15 Letter to Abbé Chevignard, July, 1905.
16 Cf. *Complete Works*, pp. 179-181.
17 *Ibid.*, p. 179.
18 Letter to Canon Angles, September, 1902.
19 Letter to Sister Agnes, June, 1902.
20 Cf. Letter to Abbé Chevignard, April, 1904.
21 Letter to Mlle. G. de Gemeaux, August, 1903.
22 Letter to Mme. Angles, February, 1904.
23 Jn 8:29.
24 Letter to Mlle. C. Blanc, October, 1906.

CHAPTER NINE

THE RELEVANCE OF A MESSAGE

To UNDERSTAND the actuality of Elizabeth's message it is necessary to review, however briefly, the reflections developed up to this point. They can all be summarized in a passage from the First Epistle of St. John: ''We ourselves have known and put our faith in God's love for ourselves. God is love and anyone who lives in love lives in God and God lives in him'' (1 Jn 4:16). Unshakable in her faith, as if she had already seen the Invisible; unshakable in her faith through an excess of love — ''We have known the love of God for us, and we have believed in it''[1] — Elizabeth did not panic or experience fear nor was she disturbed, as the apostles were when Jesus announced his departure from this world. No; she accepted in faith the words of the Master:

> *"Trust in God still, and trust in me. There are many rooms in my Father's house; if there were not, I should not have told you. I am going now to prepare a place for you, and after I have gone and prepared you a place, I shall return to take you with me, so that where I am, you may be too. You know the way to the place where I am going."*
>
> *Thomas said: "Lord, we do not know where you are going, so how can we know the way?"*

Jesus said: "I am the Way, the Truth and the Life. No one can come to the Father except through me. If you know me, you know my Father too. From this moment you know him and have seen him."

Philip said: "Lord, let us see the Father and then we shall be satisfied."

"Have I been with you all this time, Philip," said Jesus to him, "and you still do not know me? To have seen me is to have seen the Father, so how can you say, 'Let us see the Father'? Do you not believe that I am in the Father and the Father is in me? The words I say to you I do not speak as from myself: it is the Father, living in me, who is doing this work. . . Whatever you ask for in my name I will do, so that the Father may be glorified in the Son. . . If you love me you will keep my commandments. I shall ask the Father and he will give you another Advocate to be with you for ever, that Spirit of truth whom the world can never receive since it neither sees nor knows him; but you know him, because he is with you, he is in you. I will not leave you orphans; I will come back to you."[2]

For Elizabeth as for St. John, Christ, the Way to the Father, is not a way that is external to the life of man and not an arduous ascetical journey, but a loving Person who lives in and with the Father. He is, so to speak, the place of the covenant of love between God and the soul. Hence, Christ is not an abstract truth or vague life, an intellectual abstraction or cold encounter; he is the personal encounter with God by reason of his divine Person and he is the image of the Father, continuing his mediation by the mission of the Holy Spirit of love.

Elizabeth's interior life received its impetus from this essential nucleus of Christian faith and it was manifested in a twofold dimension — the vertical and the horizontal. Through the former, she was aware of the infinite love of the Father through which, in the Spirit and through the Son, she experienced a special vital relationship. Through the latter, which was a consequence and a sign of her love of God, she knew and lived the apostolic aspect of fraternal charity, though she did so behind the walls of the monastic cloister.

The centrality of her doctrine focuses on the indwelling of the Trinity, a doctrine re-echoed and confirmed in various documents of the Second Vatican Council. The Carmelite of Dijon was in a certain sense a precursor of new and original concepts of being in the Church as a contemplative and an apostle. Moreover, the fact that God was experienced by Elizabeth not in his divine unity but as a trinity of divine Persons, carries with it some important practical applications for all who have been baptized in the name of the Father and of the Son and of the Holy Spirit. It provides a new way of understanding and living the reality of the Trinity, not as an abstract concept removed from historical reality, but as distinct Persons, each one with a proper function, operating fruitfully in the hearts of believers.

In addition, the Christian life, which receives the seal of the Trinity in the reception of baptism, cannot but develop under this sign by means of a constant and progressive movement towards full and definitive union with the Most Holy Trinity. The role and function of each Person of the Trinity, and especially that of the Holy Spirit, is discernible in the interior life of the "new man."

Elizabeth's Experience Of Trinitarian Communion

THE PASCHAL MYSTERY, the last earthly action of the incarnate Word, and the mystery of ecclesial communion (i.e., adoptive filiation and fraternal brotherhood) constitute the salvific plan of God. In Elizabeth there was actuated an interpersonal communion between herself and the Father through the mediation of Christ in the Holy Spirit. God the Father revealed and gave himself through Christ in the breathing of the Holy Spirit and led Elizabeth into the ineffable mystery of love in the Trinity. This is the nucleus of the mystery of the Trinity as the Carmelite of Dijon understood and experienced it. The words of John, quoted above, were verified in her: "We ourselves have known and put our faith in God's love for ourselves. God is love and anyone who lives in love lives in God and God lives in him" (1 Jn 4:16).

Through experiencing the God who is Love, she perceives that she is incapable of containing within her interior the absolute Other. He overwhelms her because truly, "God is greater than our heart."[3]   From this springs her maternal instinct to strive to possess in her very being the divine mystery that is greater than she. Her heart responds with a total abandonment and surrender that seeks to give itself completely to him who possesses it, offering no resistance whatever to his salvific plan. In so doing, Elizabeth does no more than respond to the vocation that God meant for her from all eternity. Thus, we read in *Lumen Gentium* of Vatican Council II:

> *The followers of Christ, called by God not in virtue of their works but by his design and grace, and justified in the Lord Jesus, have been made sons of God in the baptism of faith and partakers of the divine nature, and so are truly sanctified. They must therefore hold on to and perfect in their lives that sanctification which they have received from God.*[4]

Participation in the divine nature through grace was granted Elizabeth, as to all baptized Christians, through the power of the Holy Spirit, who is the activating principle of adoptive filiation. Giving himself to her as uncreated love, he infused into her soul the theological virtues and his sevenfold gifts. He then took possession of her as a dynamic principle in order to perfect in her the identification with the Word incarnate and to lead her to intimate communion with the Father.

Thus, the mystical life that Elizabeth was called to, after the example of the Virgin Mary, was a life lived under the guidance of the Holy Spirit. Hers was the supernatural life of the spiritual man described by St. Paul, to which Elizabeth loved to refer.

Those are the ones he chose specially long ago and intended to become true images of his Son, so that his Son might be the eldest of many brothers. He called those he intended for this; those he called he justified, and with those he justified he shared his glory.[5]

Elizabeth is certain that she is among those whom God has chosen, calling her to justification and glory in conformity with the image of Christ (Gal 3:26) to be together with them the praise of glory of the Trinity.

Before the world was made, he chose us, chose us in Christ, to be holy and spotless, and to live through love in his presence, determining that we should become his adopted sons, through Jesus Christ for his own kind purposes... And it is in him that we were claimed as God's own, chosen from the beginning, under the predetermined plan of the one who guides all things as he decides by his own will; chosen to be, for his greater glory, the people who would put their hopes in Christ before he came.[6]

The salvific plan of God, which was realized in Christ, has for its primary goal the adoption of sons for the praise and glory of the Father, and this was the *leit-motif* of Elizabeth's spirituality. For Elizabeth the glory of God meant the manifestation to others, by the witness of her life, of what God is in himself and his gift of self to humanity. It is the success of his design for the human person, namely, the full realization of the individual, called to enjoy communion of life with the divine Persons.

With her soul engaged in contemplation, Elizabeth carries into act her specific charism to be the glory of the Trinity by offering herself and giving herself generously to God and to neighbor. In being occupied with God alone and in consecrating herself to him as a sacrifice of praise, she manifests certain elements — typically Carmelite — that are essential for the attainment and fruition of divine intimacy: solitude as an indispensable condition for silence, prayer as the availability of her whole life in order to listen to God, and penance as the ascetical aspect of conformation to the paschal Christ, who is the sure way for attaining intimacy with the Trinity.[7]   Solitude and silence are constitutive elements of desert spirituality and Elizabeth embraced them with determination and courage because they are so conducive to listening to God, who communicates himself to the interior of the soul. ''The Father,'' says St. John of the Cross, ''has only one word, his word, and he pronounces it in eternal silence; and it is in silence that the soul should hear it.''[8]   External silence led the young Carmelite to interior silence — silence of memory, imagination, senses and spirit — and this is the only silence that disposes the soul for an encounter with God so that she can praise and adore him. Elizabeth's prayer life comprised all of this; hers was a prayer of praise and thanksgiving, but above all an awareness and adoration of the God dwelling in her soul.

Among the various mystical aspects of Elizabeth's contemplative life perhaps one of the most important is the apostolic fruitfulness that was operative in her life style as a cloistered nun. The apostolic character of her mysticism is indeed a guarantee of the authenticity of her contemplation, which was an experiential knowledge of God as Love and of union with the entire human race. It is easy to find in Elizabeth's contemplation the vital rhythm that unites her to God and causes her to breathe a sigh of love, however painful, for the salvation of her brethren. And not only that, but her love as a spouse that causes her to be detached from self in order to be carried to the Other reflects the procession of reciprocal love between the Father and the Son that is the Holy Spirit, who never ceases to give himself to the human creature. It is an exigency of his nature as the Spirit of love. That love is a divine power which gushes forth in Elizabeth and carries her beyond the limits of her created nature, and she is unable to resist the ecstatic impulse of it. She is compelled to resort to the theological virtues infused in her soul by the Holy Spirit at baptism for they are the means by which she can respond to the uncreated love that permeates her entire being.

Precursor Of Union With God

AFTER OUR SYNTHETIC PRESENTATION of the traits of Elizabeth's spirituality, we discover that our Carmelite was a woman who far surpassed the ideas expressed in her writings. If we were to follow the spiritual path traversed by her, we would, like her, experience the love of the mystery of the Trinity. This is the guarantee of the validity and perennial value of her spiritual doctrine and also of the originality of her spiritual teaching. Now we can see it as a harbinger and forecast of what the Church would teach and live sometime in the future. In fact, the main points of Elizabeth's doctrine can be found here and there in the various documents issued by Vatican Council II. A survey of the Council texts reveals, sometimes only partially or implicitly, the basic nucleus of the spiritual teaching of Elizabeth of the Trinity.

In the *Dogmatic Constitution on the Church in the Modern World* the Council Fathers affirm: "The dignity of man rests above all on the fact that he is called to communion with God. The invitation to converse with God is addressed to man as soon as he comes into being. For if man exists it is because God has created him through love, and through love continues to hold him in existence. He cannot live fully according to truth unless he freely acknowledges that love and entrusts himself to his Creator.''[9] Such a vocation can be realized in the contemplative life of the various religious orders that the Church wants to refashion in a form adapted to the needs of modern life, with the proviso that they remain faithful to the traditions of their own religious institute.[10]   The essence of such a life consists in solitude and silence in constant prayer and intense penance. Thus, we read in the document that treats of religious life:

> *There are institutes which are entirely ordered towards contemplation, in such wise that their members give themselves over to God alone in solitude and silence, in constant prayer and willing penance. These will always have an honored place in the Mystical Body of Christ, in which ''all the members do not have the same function'' (Rm 12:4), no matter how pressing may be the needs of the active ministry. For they offer to God an exceptional sacrifice of praise, they lend luster to God's people with abundant fruits of holiness, they sway them by their example, and they enlarge the Church by their hidden apostolic fruitfulness.*[11]

If it is lived authentically, the contemplative life does have an apostolic dimension and it can thereby render an exquisite and prudent witness to the Church and to the locality in which it is lived.

> *Institutes of the contemplative life, by their prayers, penances and trials, are of the greatest importance in the conversion of souls, since it is in answer to prayer that God sends workers into this harvest (cf. Mt 9:38), opens the minds of non-Christians to hear the Gospel (cf. Ac 16:4), and makes fruitful the word of salvation in their hearts.*[12]

Indeed, contemplative charity is the soul of every apostolate, while that which sustains the life of every Christian called to holiness is fidelity to the duties of daily life. "All Christians, in the conditions, duties and circumstances of their life and through all these, will sanctify themselves more and more if they receive all things with faith from the hand of the heavenly Father and cooperate with the divine will, thus showing forth in that temporal service the love with which God has loved the world."[13]

In striving for sanctity the man who has become a new creature through baptism of the Spirit and has entered into the dialectic dynamism of the death and resurrection of the paschal Christ should strive to conform himself constantly to the image of Christ until he attains the stature of the new and perfect man.

> *All the members must be formed in his likeness, until Christ be formed in them (cf. Gal 4:19). For this reason we, who have been made like to him, who have died with him and risen with him, are taken up into the mysteries of his life, until we reign together with him (cf. Ph 3:21; 2 Tm 2:11; Ep 2:6; Col 2:12; etc.). On earth, still as pilgrims in a strange land, following in trial and in oppression the paths he trod, we are associated with his sufferings as the body with its head, suffering with him, that with him we may be glorified (cf. Rm 8:17). . .*

> *In order that we might be unceasingly renewed in him (cf. Ep 4:23), he has shared with us his Spirit who, being one and the same in head and members, gives life to, unifies and moves the whole body. Consequently, his work could be compared by the Fathers to the function that the principle of life, the soul, fulfills in the human body.[14]*

As Renewer and Purifier the Holy Spirit exercises his functions as the vital principle by the infusion of the theological virtues and his sevenfold gifts. And it is especially the Holy Spirit who gives testimony to man that he is a son of God: "The Spirit dwells in the

Church and in the hearts of the faithful as in a temple (cf. 1 Cor 3:16; 6:19). In them he prays and bears witness to their adoptive sonship (cf. Gal 4:6; Rm 8:15-16 and 26).''[15] ''So it is, united with Christ in the Church and marked with the Holy Spirit 'who is the guarantee of our inheritance' (Ep 1:14), that we are truly called and indeed are children of God (cf. 1 Jn 3:1).''[16] Through his adoptive sonship and in virtue of this sublime reality, the Christian can be led by the Spirit, through Christ's mediation, to communion with the Trinity. Thus, we read in the *Dogmatic Constitution on Divine Revelation*:

> *It pleased God, in his goodness and wisdom, to reveal himself and to make known the mystery of his will (cf. Ep 1:9). His will was that men should have access to the Father, through Christ, the Word made flesh, in the Holy Spirit, and thus become sharers in the divine nature (cf. Ep 2:18; 2 P 1:4). By this revelation, then, the invisible God (cf. Col 1:15; 1 Tm 1:17), from the fullness of his love, addresses men as his friends (cf. Ex 33:11; Jn 15:14-15), and moves among them (cf. Ba 3:38), in order to invite and receive them into his own company.*[17]

In man's sublime vocation to communion with the Trinity the mystery of Christ has an important function and Vatican Council II has placed it at the center of Christian formation. ''In reality it is only in the mystery of the Word made flesh that the mystery of man truly becomes clear. . . The Church believes that Christ, who died and was raised for the sake of all, can show man the way and can strengthen him through the Spirit in order to be worthy of his destiny; nor is there any other name under heaven given among men by which they can be saved (cf. Ac 4:12).''[18] The mystery of the dead and resurrected Christ who vivifies us through the sacraments, and especially through the Eucharist, is the root and the hinge of every spiritual life. But there is more; by his incarnate presence, which enabled him to share the human condition,[19] Christ effects a gradual and progressive consecration of earthly reality, directing all of it to the service of mankind and the glory of God.

The Word of God, through whom all things were made, became man and dwelt among men: a perfect man, he entered world history, taking that history into himself and recapitulating it. . . Christ's example in dying for us sinners teaches us that we must carry the cross, which the flesh and the world inflict on the shoulders of all who seek after peace and justice. Constituted Lord by his resurrection and given all authority in heaven and on earth, Christ is now at work in the hearts of men by the power of his Spirit. . . But of all the Spirit makes free men, who are ready to put aside love of self and integrate earthly resources into human life, in order to reach out to that future day when mankind itself will become an offering accepted by God.[20]

Therefore, the prayers and efforts of men as Church are directed to the full realization of Christ's activity as Head of the Mystical Body, both in the spiritual and the temporal orders.[21] "Thus the Church prays and likewise labors so that into the People of God, the Body of the Lord and the Temple of the Holy Spirit, may pass the fullness of the whole world, and that in Christ, the Head of all things, all honor and glory may be rendered to the Creator, the Father of the universe."[22]

In this global vision of man redeemed by Christ and raised to the level of God, the Council recognizes sanctity as the perfection of charity in the total mystery of Christ. Christ's gift of love is the essence of sanctity and Christ has revealed to us that "God is love" (1 Jn 4:8). He likewise taught us that the fundamental precept of human perfection, and hence also of the transformation of the world, is the new commandment of love. Therefore those who believe in love are certain that the pathway of love is open to all men and that the intense efforts to establish a universal brotherhood are not in vain. Moreover, one is cautioned not to walk the path of love only in regard to great things, but in the ordinary events of daily life.

Apostolic charity is not the function of priests alone, whose task it is to gather God's family in Christ and bring it to the Father. It is the duty of the entire Church, of all the People of God; all have an obligation to extend the kingdom of God on earth. "The Church was founded to spread the kingdom of Christ over all the earth for the glory of God the Father, to make all men partakers in redemption and salvation, and through them to establish the right relationship of the entire world to Christ. Every activity of the Mystical Body with this in view goes by the name of 'apostolate'; the Church exercises it through all its members, though in various ways. In fact, the Christian vocation is, of its nature, a vocation to the apostolate as well."[23]   The apostolate is therefore a primary duty flowing from one's love of God and neighbor, to be exercised in conformity with one's vocation and state of life.

All of the foregoing basic teachings resemble closely what Elizabeth lived and wrote in her monastery of the Carmel of Dijon. It is relatively easy to see the comparison between the teaching of Vatican Council II and the doctrine of Elizabeth, but the practical consequences for one's daily Christian life are even more evident.

Communion With The Trinity In The Christian Life

INTIMATE COMMUNION with the Trinity is not something exclusive to Elizabeth and a few mystics. It is possible for any Christian who is disposed for God to act in him. The message conveyed by the mystic of Dijon and confirmed by Vatican Council II could easily be seen as absurd because of the commitment it demands in order to be lived fully. But this does not mean that the Christian is excluded because he is not called to so lofty and elevated an experience. On the contrary, precisely because he is a baptized Christian he is called to communion with the Trinity by the fact of being reborn in water and the Holy Spirit.

The sacrament of baptism is related not only to the death and resurrection of Christ but also to the mystery of the Trinity. In fact, it is through baptism that the three divine Persons take up their abode in the soul of the baptized person, and they call that person to a sharing of divine life and the work of progressive sanctification. That is why the baptized is a person who has been sealed or stamped by the Trinity, who want to take possession of him who has been resurrected from spiritual death and raised to sonship with God. This adoptive sonship is the effect of a gratuitous action of God; it springs from the love of the Father (1 Jn 3:1), is ratified by the gift of the Holy Spirit (Rm 8:15), and in its development tends to conform the individual to the image of the only-begotten Son (Rm 8:29). Thus, the sacrament of baptism establishes an intimate and profound relationship of love between the Christian and the Trinity. He is no longer a servant but a friend and a son, and he can call God by the name of ''Father'' (Gal 4:5-6).

The birth to a new life in the Spirit is the beginning of a long road that associates the Christian with the life of Christ. In fact, the Christian life involves a divesting of the ''old man'' and a putting on of the new man who is Christ (Gal 3:27). He is called to live his entire life in Christ (Col 2:6), to be more and more assimilated to Christ (Col 3:10), and to be rooted in him who is the image of the invisible God (Col 1:9). Achieving this, he will not be able to do otherwise than state with St. Paul: ''I live now, not I, but Christ lives in me'' (Gal 2:20).

Experiencing at this point the mystery of communion with the Trinity but not yet having achieved fully the transforming union with God who is Love, the Christian progressively follows the steps of love under the constant guidance of the Holy Spirit. Having been regenerated by the love of the Father (1 Jn 3:1), he receives an abundance of the love of God from the Holy Spirit

(Rm 5:5), who leads him to live in union with the Father and with his Son Jesus Christ (1 Jn 1:3). Thus is the plan of God realized in man: to lead him to an experience of blessed life in him. "For God has called man, and still calls him, to cleave with all his being to him in sharing forever a life that is divine and free from all decay."[24] Such a sharing of life finds its full completion in the incarnation, passion, death, resurrection and glorification of Christ. Only in him, with him and through him is it possible to share in divine life, to attain to *koinonia* with the Triune God.

> *Human nature, by the very fact that it was assumed, not absorbed, in him, has been raised in us also to a dignity beyond compare. For, by his incarnation, he, the Son of God, has in a certain way united himself with each man. He worked with human hands, he thought with a human mind. He acted with a human will, and with a human heart he loved. Born of the Virgin Mary, he has truly been made one of us, like to us in all things except sin.*[25]

In simple language and in a manner accessible to all, Jesus, the Son of Mary, speaks to man about his Father and ours. He speaks also of his love for man that is so great that he will give his life for the salvation of mankind and thereby satisfy all the needs of humanity because such is the will of his Father. Jesus is the eternal Word of the Father, announced throughout the centuries, who was spoken in time for the salvation of all those who believe in him and practice what he taught.

> *At various times in the past and in various ways, God spoke to our ancestors through the prophets; but in our own time, the last days, he has spoken to us through his Son. . . He is the radiant light of God's glory and the perfect copy of his nature, sustaining the universe by his powerful command;*

and now that he has destroyed the defilement of sin, he has
gone to take his place in heaven at the right hand of divine
Majesty.[26]

Jesus continues to speak to mankind and in the measure that man
makes an existential response, his life can become a symphony of
love that becomes the praise and glory of the Father, the Son and
the Holy Spirit, until such time as hope is fulfilled and the veil is
lifted. Only then will they ''see him face to face, and his name will
be written on their foreheads. It will never be night again and they
will not need lamplight or sunlight, because the Lord God will be
shining on them. They will reign for ever and ever.''[27]   The
blessed will reign in a timeless region where there is no space or
place, in an eternal springtime beyond all seasons, basking in the
radiant light of the unique Sun of Love. There the beatified, their
white garments washed in the Blood of the Lamb, will dwell in an
ecstasy of everlasting prayer.

From what has been said it should be evident that the Trinity is
not simply an object of study or possessed by only a few chosen
souls; it is the center, the focal point, of the Christian life. In the
history of Israel, which is likewise the history of every Christian, in
every circumstance of joy or suffering, one can perceive the
presence of God the Father who liberated and saved, gathering
sinful man in his forgiving love whenever he was disposed to
accept God's love. And in order to carry out this plan which was
ordained from all eternity, the Father, in his infinite love, made
himself visible and tangible in the person of his incarnate Son.
Hence, the whole history of Jesus, the humanized Word — his life,
his words, his actions — are not only for the instruction of mankind
but are above all a continuous affirmation of his divine and human
natures which are the channel of grace for reaching the Father. In
this sense the Word is Savior, the sacrament of encounter between
the Father and human creatures.

At the conclusion of his earthly mission, the incarnate Word sent to the community of believers the Paraclete, the consoling Spirit. He lives in the Church and vivifies it from within; he fosters its growth and leads it to full communion with the Father through Jesus Christ. It is the task of the Holy Spirit to restore all creation to the bosom of the Father, and hence to effect the fulfillment of the vocation of humanity to know the Father and him whom the Father sent. To put it in other words, his work is to insert humanity into the *koinonia* of love among the three divine Persons, thus constituting a divine family.

All our faith, the Christian life, the life of the Church, sealed as they are by the character of the Holy Spirit, are profoundly involved in this great mystery of love. The Sign of the Cross reminds the Christian of the mystery that dwells in his soul through grace, so that he can exclaim with St. Augustine:

O Lord our God, we believe in you, the Father and the Son and the Holy Spirit. Because the Truth would not say: "Go baptize all nations in the name of the Father and of the Son and of the Holy Spirit" (Mt 28:19) unless there was a Trinity. Nor would you, O Lord God, have commanded us to be baptized in the name of him who is not the Lord God. And the divine voice would not have said: "Hear, O Israel, the Lord thy God is one God" (Dt 6:4) unless you were a Trinity in such wise as to be one Lord and God. And if you, O God, were yourself the Father and yourself the Son, your Word Jesus Christ, and your Gift, the Holy Spirit, we would not read in Scripture: "God sent his Son" (Gal 4:5), nor would you, the Only-begotten, say of the Holy Spirit: "Whom the Father will send in my name" (Jn 14:26) and "Whom I will send to you from the Father" (Jn 15:26).

Directing my attention to this rule of faith as much as I have been able, and as much as you have made me able, I have sought you and have desired to see with my understanding that which I have believed; and I have argued and labored much.

O Lord, my God, my only hope, hearken to me and see to it that I do not cease to seek you because of weariness, but that I may "always ardently seek thy face" (Ps 104:4). Give me the strength to seek you, you who have enabled me to find you and have given me the hope of finding you more and more. My strength and my weakness are in your sight; sustain the one and heal the other. My knowledge and my ignorance are in your sight; where you have opened to me, receive me as I enter; where you have closed to me, open when I knock. Make me remember you, understand you, and love you. Increase these things in me until you renew me entirely. . .

Speaking of you, the wise man stated in his book (which is called Ecclesiasticus [Sirach]): *"We could say much more and still fall short; to put it concisely, 'He is all' " (Si 43:29). When, therefore, we shall have arrived in your presence, these many words that we speak and still fall short will cease and you alone will remain "all in all" (1 Cor 15:29). And without end we shall say one word in praising you in a single impulse, having been made one thing with you, O Lord, one God, God the Trinity.*[28]

FOOTNOTES

1 Col 1:12. Cf. Elizabeth of the Trinity, *Complete Works*, tr. A. Kane, O.C.D., ICS Publications, Washington, D.C. 1984, Vol. I, p. 145.
2 Jn 14:1-18, *passim.*
3 1 Jn 3:20.
4 *Vatican Council II: the Conciliar and Post Conciliar Documents*, ed. A. Flannery, O.P., Costello Publishing Company, Northport, N.Y., 1975, *Lumen Gentium*, no. 40.
5 Rm 8:29-30.
6 Ep 1:4-5; 11-12.
7 Cf. *Perfectae Caritatis*, no. 7.
8 St. John of the Cross, *Maxims on Love*, no. 21.
9 *Gaudium et Spes*, no. 19.
10 Cf. *Ad Gentes Divinitus*, no. 18.
11 *Perfectae Caritatis*, no. 7.
12 *Ad Gentes Divinitus*, no. 40.
13 *Lumen Gentium*, no. 41.
14 *Ibid.*, no. 7.
15 *Ibid.*, no. 4.
16 *Ibid.*, no. 48.
17 *Dei Verbum*, no. 2.
18 *Gaudium et Spes*, nos. 22 and 10.
19 *Ibid.*, no. 22.
20 *Ibid.*, no. 38.
21 Cf. *Apostolicam Actuositatem*, no. 5.
22 *Lumen Gentium*, no. 17.
23 *Apostolicam Actuositatem*, no. 2.
24 *Gaudium et Spes*, no. 18.
25 *Ibid.*, no. 22.
26 Heb 1:1-3.
27 Rv 22:4-5.
28 St. Augustine, *De Trinitate*, Book 15, chap. 28.

CONCLUSION

IN HER JOURNEY to sanctity Elizabeth seems to have been firmly committed from the first moment to a search for the mystery of the Trinity, concretized in contemplation. From the very start she was convinced that she had been called to exist as the praise of glory on behalf of her brethren. Hers was a rich experience of both contemplative prayer and openness to the world. The basis of her pilgrimage toward the absolute who is God can be found in her desire for interior enrichment based on the examples of experience, praised by mystics of all times, but even more in the need to preserve the thread of contemplative spirituality inherited from Teresa of Jesus and John of the Cross, a spirituality that is lived bit by bit in the solitude of Carmel. Along the stages of this journey, which she travelled with great care, Elizabeth always endeavored to discover God's will for her as she strove for communion with the Trinity. And once discerning God's will, she applied herself to it with great dedication. Her program of love was well scheduled and it followed the phases established by God from all eternity.

Destined from all eternity and called by name in time — Elizabeth, house of God — the young Carmelite tried with all her strength to live up to the name that had been given her by God: to be the praise of the glory of the Trinity in purity and sanctity of life. Such is the itinerary she followed with zeal and great care. So ardently did she pursue her quest that she quickly arrived at the ecstasy of communion with the divine. Knowing God through his sacred humanity and in faith, she wanted to possess him completely. The virtue of hope aroused in her was not an apathetic waiting but the consuming ardor of her whole being, animated by love, to attain to full realization of divine intimacy with the Trinity.

In the weaving of this tapestry by God and Elizabeth — the two partners in this marvelous love story — Mary was the model, the way, the inspiration and an efficacious aid for the attainment of the desired goal. The Virgin of listening and recollection was the secure anchor to which the young Carmelite attached herself, not to remain fixed in the calm waters of an illusory port of arrival, but to continue together with her on the journey to divine union. It was a long and painful journey because it demanded of Elizabeth that she be conformed to Christ on the cross, with whom she felt herself as a co-redemptrix and mediatrix. Not only that, but through Christ's mediation in his paschal mystery she penetrated the mystery of the Trinity.

To attain this goal she was invited, not as a spectator but as a protagonist, to pass through the desert, to silence her senses, emotions and spirit, to die in order to rise again and then, living a new life according to the Spirit, through Christ, to share in the sweet and ineffable intimacy of God the Father. All of this involved an active purgation followed by a passive purification which was much more demanding and was worked in her by the Holy Spirit. Refined in the crucible of suffering, she was transformed and vivified by faith, hope and charity, to the point of becoming a worthy dwelling place for the Trinity.

The indwelling of the Trinity was not for Elizabeth an object of theological reflection but a vivid and vital experience during which she re-lived the reality of her baptism. She was deified, as it were, so that she no longer operated on the natural plane but did all things in a supernatural manner. And if she was divinized by the Holy Spirit, it was because he wanted to make her an object of rejoicing and infinite love on the part of the Trinity. In this way the entire life of Elizabeth, which no longer belonged to her, became an incessant praise and adoration of the triune God dwelling in the holy temple of her soul.

Such an experience of loving contemplation, although totally interior and within the walls of a cloister, is fruitful and beneficial for the life and expansion of the Church, because it was authentic and was anchored in the living waters of the divine Absolute. Through her dynamic contemplative prayer Elizabeth rendered to the Church and to all mankind a fruitful apostolic service.

Here we can draw the contemporary relevance from the message of Elizabeth, who knew how to live her daily life hidden with Christ in the mystery of communion with the Trinity. The relevance is all the more evident when one realizes that everything that the young Carmelite wrote and lived was not the result of some intellectual musing but the result of her own experience, an experience that was related to the Church and based on the Gospel teaching. In delineating her spiritual portrait in the preceding pages we have at the same time manifested the actuality of her message, which is at once evangelical, ecclesial and Christian.

As one can see, we do not find in Elizabeth any extraordinary mystical phenomena as in the case of St. Teresa of Avila and St. John of the Cross. Herein lies the secret of her sanctity and the heroism of her life — to be faithful moment by moment to her baptismal vocation which was ratified by her religious profession. Such fidelity connotes a total and generous dedication to the paschal Christ, who is the way to the Father through the Holy Spirit to the praise and glory of the Trinity and for the benefit of all mankind. It all has its beginning, basis and confirmation in the Word of God on which she meditated and which she assimilated, and then carried out in her daily life so far as it applied to her vocation. All this was done with heroic simplicity, in faith, hope and love.

A humble and simple Carmelite, a disciple of St. Paul, strongly attached to the spiritual tradition of Carmel, Elizabeth, by the testimony of her life, offers a pressing invitation to traverse as she did the pathways of divine grace in order to reach union with God. The charism that was proper to her, she continues to exercise even after her death, as she had forseen and predicted. Even now it echoes in the heart of anyone who knows how to listen and catch the echo of a message that is an ecclesial experience of theological interiority in the dialogue of prayer, through the mediation of Christ and configuration to the mystery of his death and resurrection, through the power of the Holy Spirit.